C000005482

This is a superb book! Punchy yet p
issues of both the church and conte
though never superficial; challenging yet simultaneously
encouraging; theologically judicious and pastorally sensitive – all
the kind of qualities we have come to expect from Vaughan
Roberts. It does what it says on the strapline, presenting 'The
challenge of 1 Corinthians for the twenty-first-century church',
and I am delighted to commend most highly *True Spirituality*.
Dr Steve Brady, Principal, Moorlands College, Christchurch

1 Corinthians is a long letter and deals with a number of, at first
sight, self-contained problems. Consequently, many of us will
know parts of the letter without really having a grasp of what lay
behind these issues and what was really going on in the church in
Corinth. That's where this book is so helpful. Four things are
worth noting. First, it is very accessible, written in an inviting and
well-illustrated style. Second, it is careful and thorough. Within
the confines of a shortish book, complex issues are dealt with
skilfully and difficult passages are not neglected. Third, it is very
thoughtfully applied. The lines between first-century Corinth and
the twenty-first-century reader are wisely drawn and there are
challenges for all. Fourth, while *True Spirituality* examines each
part of 1 Corinthians in turn, the reader is never allowed to lose
sight of the big issues that hold the whole of the book together.
I would recommend this excellent book for anyone who wants to
study 1 Corinthians or wants to think biblically about what true
spirituality looks like in ordinary life. The addition of very helpful
Bible study questions at the end of each chapter invites readers to
look carefully at the book for themselves or with others.
Andy Gemmill, Scottish Cornhill Training Course

True Spirituality is worth the asking price for chapter 6 alone, and
Vaughan has done us a great service in expounding the timeless
truths of 1 Corinthians and showing us their contemporary
application. Here we have a heart-warming and winsome counter

to our increasingly relativistic, feminized and permissive culture, and a timely reminder that true power is found in the weakness of the cross.

Carrie Sandom, women's worker at St John's, Tunbridge Wells and part-time lecturer at the Cornhill Training Course in London

TRUE
SPIRITUALITY

To David and Susie Fletcher
on their ruby wedding anniversary,
29 August 2010

VAUGHAN ROBERTS

TRUE SPIRITUALITY

The challenge of 1 Corinthians for the twenty-first-century church

ivp

INTER-VARSITY PRESS
Norton Street, Nottingham NG7 3HR, England
Email: ivp@ivpbooks.com
Website: www.ivpbooks.com

© Vaughan Roberts, 2011

Unless otherwise stated, Scripture quotations are taken from the Holy
Bible, New International Version. Copyright © 1973, 1978, 1984 by
International Bible Society. Used by permission of Hodder & Stoughton,
a division of Hodder Headline Ltd. All rights reserved. 'NIV' is a trademark
of International Bible Society. UK trademark number 1448790.

Scripture quotations marked ESV are taken from The Holy Bible, English
Standard Version, published by HarperCollins Publishers, copyright © 2001
by Crossway Bibles, a division of Good News Publishers. Used by
permission.

First published 2011

British Library Cataloguing in Publication Data
A catalogue record for this book is available from the British Library.

ISBN: 978–1–84474–518–0

Set in Dante 12/15pt
Typeset in Great Britain by CRB Associates, Potterhanworth, Lincolnshire
Printed and bound in Great Britain by Ashford Colour Press Ltd, Gosport,
Hampshire

*Inter-Varsity Press publishes Christian books that are true to the Bible and that
communicate the gospel, develop discipleship and strengthen the church for its
mission in the world.*

*Inter-Varsity Press is closely linked with the Universities and Colleges Christian
Fellowship, a student movement connecting Christian Unions in universities and
colleges throughout Great Britain, and a member movement of the International
Fellowship of Evangelical Students. Website: www.uccf.org.uk*

Contents

Acknowledgments

I have benefitted greatly from preaching early versions of this material at St Ebbe's Oxford, Word Alive (South Africa), New Word Alive, the Keswick Convention and the South Central Ministry Training Course, and want to thank those who gave me these opportunities. I am particularly grateful to Lucy Bannister, Clare Heath-Whyte, Annabel Heywood, Neil Jeffers and Pete Wilkinson for commenting on the manuscript, and to Lucy Bannister for her typing.

Paul stresses in 1 Corinthians that true spirituality must never be an individual preoccupation, but is to be worked out in fellowship with other believers in a local church. It is my privilege to be a member of St Ebbe's, Oxford, and I am full of gratitude for the past and present members of the church family who have meant so much to me for over twenty years. They have taught me more about what true spirituality looks like in practice than I could ever put down in these pages. Without their encouragement to me to keep writing, and the gentle badgering of a few friends when I was flagging, this book would not have been written.

Although I only read Francis Schaeffer's excellent *True Spirituality*[1] while I was writing this book, and am not sure I had heard of it when I first preached a sermon series with the same name, it is likely that it was somewhere in my sub-conscious, so I gladly credit him with the title.

Introduction

A spiritual crisis

The first major crisis in my Christian life came about a year after my conversion. I had come to Christ shortly before leaving school, simply through reading Matthew's Gospel. It was as if the Lord Jesus walked off the pages and into my life, filling me with a deep assurance of forgiveness and a conviction that I could never be the same again. In those early months I grew rapidly in understanding my new faith and strove hard to live it out. It was a honeymoon period in which I enjoyed a peace and joy I had never known before; but then came the crisis.

Shortly after leaving school I went as a volunteer helper to a holiday centre for the disabled. There I met two Christians who were roughly the same age as me. It was the first time I had got to know believers from very different backgrounds from mine, and I delighted in the fellowship we enjoyed as we prayed together and tried to witness to the guests and other volunteers. All went well until my new friends began to describe some experiences they had received and urged me to ask God to do the same for me. They told me that I had received Christ, but that the Holy Spirit was still not living in my life. If only I would open myself up to him, then I would be able to know a far greater power in my Christian life and a closer walk with Christ.

I was confused by what they said but I certainly did not want to miss out on anything from God, so I prayed earnestly to receive the experiences they had told me about. When nothing happened I prayed again, but still with no effect. The joy I had previously known deserted me, and I was filled with spiritual insecurity. Was it true that I had never received the Holy Spirit? Was there a whole plane of Christian experience that I was missing out on? If so, was that because God did not love me as much as he loved my friends? Had I not been praying earnestly enough? Or was it possible that my friends were misguided and were pointing me in the wrong direction? How could I tell?

True spirituality: a contemporary issue

The questions I was grappling with were a particular manifestation of an issue that has an urgent relevance: what is the nature of true spirituality? Perhaps no other subject causes greater confusion and, sadly, division among Christians today. What does it mean to be a truly spiritual Christian? New trends frequently sweep through the Christian world, which can give the impression that those who do not embrace their teaching and practices are second-class disciples. None of us wants to miss out on all that God is doing, so our ears prick up when we hear of some movement, teaching or personality claiming to offer a new work of God's Spirit. But how can we discern what is really from God?

I am very grateful to an older Christian who came alongside me during my spiritual crisis and pointed me in the right direction. He told me not to focus on dramatic experiences, clever arguments or the personalities of my friends, although they were undoubtedly sincere and passionate, but rather to look to the teaching of the Bible. Taking his advice, I read the whole New Testament and measured what I had been told against it. The result was both reassuring and challenging. I saw no evidence in the New Testament that there are two classes of Christians, spiritual and unspiritual, or that some believers have progressed into a different sphere of spirituality through a particular experience. It became clear to me that all people are spiritually dead by nature and can only become Christians, or stay Christians, by the miraculous life-giving work of the Holy Spirit within them. All Christians are spiritual because, as Paul puts it, 'If anyone does not have the Spirit of Christ, they do not belong to Christ' (Romans 8:9).

Paul's letter to the Colossians was especially helpful to me. The apostle counters those in Colosse who claimed that it was not enough simply to know Christ and taught that there was a deeper knowledge of God that could be enjoyed by those who also embraced extra revelation, experiences and practices. These words in particular leapt out at me and gave me great reassurance: 'For in Christ all the fullness of the Deity lives in bodily form, and in Christ you have been brought to fullness' (Colossians 2:9–10). If, by coming to Christ, I had already entered into a relationship with the One who is the fullness of God, how could there be more of God to be received from some other source? But along with the encouragement came a profound challenge: I had received so much from God in Christ by the Spirit, but was I living in the light of all that I had received? Was I keeping 'in step with the Spirit' (Galatians 5:25), delighting in fellowship with Christ, resisting sin, walking in holiness and taking every opportunity to build up others and point unbelievers to Christ?

True spirituality: a Corinthian issue

The goal of this book is to help Christians who are seeking to discern the nature of true spirituality, by applying the advice my mentor gave to me and looking to the Bible for answers. We will be focusing on Paul's first letter to the Corinthians, because it directly addresses our subject. Paul had been used by God to establish a church in Corinth, which was a major port and commercial centre in what is now southern Greece, during his eighteen-month stay there in his second missionary journey in the early 50s AD (see Acts 18). He wrote 1 Corinthians about two or three years after his departure to respond to developments in the church that were causing concern. It seems that the Corinthians prided themselves on being very 'spiritual' (a word that appears twelve times in the letter, more than in the rest of the New Testament put together). Other words that are often repeated also seem to be qualities they admired and believed they possessed: 'wisdom', 'knowledge' and 'power'.

Corinthian buzzwords[1]	
Spiritual	2:13, 14, 15; 3:1; 9:11; 10:3–4; 12:1; 14:1, 37; 15:44, 46
Wisdom	1:17, 19, 20, 21, 22, 24, 30; 2:1, 4, 5, 6, 7, 13; 3:19; 12:8
Knowledge	1:5; 8:1, 7, 10, 11; 12:8; 13:2, 8; 14:6
Power	1:18, 24; 2:4–5; 4:19, 20; 5:4; 6:14; 12:10; 15:24, 43, 56

The Corinthians really thought they had arrived in these areas and that they had left Paul behind. In contrast to them, he was unspiritual, ignorant, weak and foolish. The apostle writes a strongly corrective letter, not simply to defend his reputation but also to restore them to true Christian faith. He picks up the words they use themselves and is basically saying,

'The knowledge, power and wisdom you claim to have are not the real thing. What you call spirituality isn't spirituality at all, it's worldly. You're being directed by the mindset and principles of the non-Christian world around you rather than by the Holy Spirit.'

That challenge is not just for the Corinthians; it also has a direct application to Christians today. It is striking how very Corinthian the twenty-first-century church is. The buzzwords that had such currency in Corinth still appear frequently in book blurbs and conference brochures today. We value exactly the same qualities and yet we often have very inadequate understandings of them. Paul's appeal to the Corinthians is God's appeal to us. We also need to repent of inadequate and worldly understandings of what it means to live by the Spirit, and instead embrace true spirituality.

A challenge for today

The approach I adopt as we study 1 Corinthians is expository rather than topical. By that I mean that I am not, first and foremost, coming to the text with a fixed set of questions on particular contemporary topics and looking to see what answers it gives. I am rather starting with the text and seeing what issues and questions it raises for us, which may differ from the ones with which we began. To understand what the Holy Spirit is saying to us through this letter in the twenty-first century, we must begin by asking what he was saying through Paul to the Corinthians in the first century. That will require us to study the text carefully. There will not be space for a detailed discussion of every verse, but I am aiming to draw out the major themes. (For a more detailed look at the text I would especially recommend David Jackman's *Let's Study 1 Corinthians*,[2] or the longer commentary by David Garland.[3])

You will gain most from this book if you read the relevant section of 1 Corinthians before each chapter and then keep it open. The Bible study questions at the end of each chapter are designed to help you individually and in groups to look more deeply into the passages and think further about how they apply today.

Some of the issues Paul addresses in 1 Corinthians, such as whether or not to eat food sacrificed to idols, may seem alien to us, but the principles are profoundly relevant. The sovereign God, who by his Holy Spirit ensured the Bible writers wrote exactly what he wanted them to write, always intended that Paul's letter to a particular group of Christians in one particular place and time would be his living word for all generations. As we study 1 Corinthians, we will hear God's word to us today, bringing both encouragement and challenge, whether our temptation is towards a super-spirituality which claims more from God than we should expect, or a sub-spirituality which is so nervous of excess that it contents itself with far less than God wants to give us. In our desire to be spiritual, we too are in danger of substituting the vibrant heart of our faith with a pale echo of the world. In correcting the Corinthians, Paul challenges us too and calls us back to true spirituality.

1. TRUE SPIRITUALITY
focuses on Christ's cross, not on human wisdom

(1 Corinthians 1 – 2)

Longing for spiritual power

I recently went to lunch in an Oxford University college with a member of our congregation, who introduced me as his pastor to a professor sitting opposite. To my surprise, the professor asked immediately if I believed in God – I would have hoped that this was obvious from my job! When I told him that I did, he was politely scornful, clearly regarding me as intellectually simplistic and naive. I confess that at the time I was reluctant to respond by talking about Christ; I longed to be able to produce something more obviously powerful, such as a dramatic miracle or a knock-down philosophical argument for the existence of God.

All of us feel weak and foolish as Christians at times. It is hard not to feel weak when we look at the strident atheism, advancing secularism, apathetic spiritual ignorance and increasing strength of Islam in our society. Even closer to home, we are bound to feel weak when we find that we are the only believer in our family, office or sports team. And we will certainly feel foolish when friends laugh at us for our outdated morality or colleagues dismiss our beliefs as narrow-minded, fundamentalist nonsense. We long for the eyes of those around us to be opened so that they too can come to know God through Christ. However, it can be very hard to believe that could happen, especially when we remember God's chosen means to bring it about: the proclamation of the gospel of Christ crucified.

The world's rejection of the cross

Non-Christians have never been impressed by the cross. Archaeologists discovered some second-century graffiti in Rome making fun of a young man bowing down before a figure on a cross, which was drawn with the head of a donkey. Beside this is the caption: 'Alexamenos worships God!' His friends clearly thought it was ridiculous that he should be foolish enough to worship as a god a man who had been executed as a common criminal.[1] Still today, there are those who are scornful or dismissive of 'crosstianity'. They can understand a version of Christianity which focuses on the moral teaching of Jesus, but have no time for those who retain the emphasis on Christ as Saviour through his sacrificial death. Others are simply mystified. Talk of Christ's agonizing death being anything other than a tragic failure makes no sense to them.

In a world that regards the message of Christ crucified as weak and foolish, it will always be tempting for Christians to look elsewhere for the power and wisdom we feel we need to impress others. Our attention can so easily shift from the message of the Bible, with its focus on the saving work of Christ through the cross, to other preoccupations. This development will often be justified as the result of the Spirit's leading or an increase in spiritual maturity, but in reality it is prompted by the mindset of the non-Christian world. Paul's teaching in 1 Corinthians 1 – 2 makes it very clear that true spiritual power and wisdom are found in Christ and the message of the cross.

A good test, therefore, of any movement or message that claims to be spiritual is to ask, 'Does this point me to the crucified Christ and encourage me to grow in knowledge and love of him, to serve him and imitate him?' If not, it does not come from the Holy Spirit, however impressive it may appear. We must be on our guard against any departure from a focus on Christ and the cross, whether it is caused by a deliberate decision or a gradual drift which flows from a form of spiritual amnesia.

Spiritual amnesia

After some introductory words, Paul begins his letter by expressing his concern about reports he had heard of the divisions in the Corinthian church: 'My brothers and sisters, some from Chloe's household have informed me that there are quarrels among you. What I mean is this: One of you says, "I follow Paul"; another, "I follow Apollos"; another, "I follow Cephas"; still another, "I follow Christ."' (1 Corinthians 1:11–12).

Travelling philosophers were common in Greek society, each proclaiming their particular brand of wisdom for life. Those with academic pretensions would attach themselves to one of these and to the school of philosophy they represented. It was a form of one-upmanship, with different groups arguing for the superiority of their way of thinking and intellectual heroes. What shocked Paul so much was that this worldly factionalism had entered the Corinthian church.

There is no hint in the letter as to what the different groups stood for. As far as we can tell, Paul, Apollos and Cephas (Peter) did not differ on any significant theological question. In fact, Paul stresses in 1 Corinthians 3 that God worked both through him, in planting the church, and through Apollos, who succeeded the apostle as its leader, in establishing it (3:6). It is most likely, therefore, that the factions in Corinth were divided, not by doctrine, but by mindset; instead of focusing on Christ they exalted human leaders, adopted them as heroes and placed them on pedestals. Paul is horrified: 'I appeal to you, brothers and sisters, in the name of our Lord Jesus Christ, that all of you agree with one another in what you say and that there be no divisions among you, but that you be perfectly united in mind and thought' (1:10).

We can imagine the different groups in the church: PPT (Pauline Preaching Trust) and ARM (Apollos Renewal Ministries), each with its own office with posters of the great leader on the walls and piles of photographs ready to be sent to donors. They assumed they would be flattered: 'We've read all your books, Paul, and downloaded every sermon; we're even thinking of calling our church St Paul's. You'd like that, wouldn't you?' But Paul is far from impressed; the Corinthians focused on their heroes, Paul, Apollos and Cephas, but he wants to bring them back to Christ alone. Jesus Christ is mentioned eleven times in the first nine verses of the letter. It is likely that 'I follow Christ' in 1:12 is not a reference to a fourth group, but rather Paul's indignant response to the other personality cults: 'You follow Apollos, Cephas and even me, but as for me, I follow Christ – and so should you.'

Paul took the factions in Corinth very seriously, because they were showing symptoms of spiritual amnesia. They had forgotten the power of Paul's message of Christ crucified, through which they had been converted, and had chosen instead to focus on a corrupted version of Christianity that fitted better with the worldly ways of thinking that were popular. They thought that by so doing they had grown in power and wisdom, but in fact they had forfeited both. In 1 Corinthians 1 – 2, the apostle corrects their thinking by stressing two important truths:

1. True power is found in weakness.
2. True wisdom is received by revelation.

1. True power is found in weakness (1:18 – 2:5)

After Paul had left them, the Corinthians began to feel that his understated style of ministry and his message, which focused on Christ's cross, was too weak to make much of an impact on sophisticated Corinth. They were increasingly drawn to the emerging leaders in the church who had more in common with the wisdom teachers who were so popular in the Greek world and gave people what they demanded: clever arguments and impressive oratory (that is, the way an idea was presented was as important as the idea itself). No doubt a personality cult attached itself to the most able Christian preachers, as it did to the best travelling philosophers, who could gather large audiences and receive high fees.

Superficially it must have looked as if these new leaders in the Corinthian church were brilliantly successful. Perhaps their congregations were overflowing, and the world had begun to take notice of them: they had become personalities with the first-century equivalents of their own newspaper columns and a regular slot on a television discussion programme. They appeared to be far more powerful than Paul, whose message of Christ crucified had been dismissed by most in Corinth; but the apostle urged the Corinthians not to be taken in, for God's understanding of power is very different from the world's. By adopting human wisdom, these new leaders had in fact forfeited God's power. As Paul himself reminded them, he had been commissioned 'to preach the gospel – not with wisdom and eloquence, lest the cross of Christ be emptied of its power' (1:17).

The weakness of the cross

The cross, as we have already seen, has always attracted strong responses. I remember one brilliant student exclaiming contemptuously, 'That's ridiculous', after I had explained that we can only be acceptable to God because Jesus Christ died for sinners on the cross to take the punishment we deserved. Another clergyman told me why he and others had so strongly opposed a church plant we had started: 'The truth is, Vaughan,' he said, 'we hate your theology.' He was speaking, above all, about the message of the cross. The Bible's teaching that we all deserve God's judgment for our sin, and that Christ's death as a substitute is our only hope, was deeply offensive to him.

While some dismiss the cross, others know that they owe everything to it. Our church recently baptized fifteen people in the River Thames. They were a diverse group: a few raised in atheistic China, one from the local council estate and some brilliant young British students, yet all spoke of how they had been transformed by the same message of Christ crucified. As Paul puts it, 'The message of the cross is foolishness to those who are perishing, but to us who are being saved it is the power of God' (1:18).

The power of the cross

What is our strategy in the huge task of seeking to win our friends and neighbours for Christ and reaching out to our nation and the wider world? Churches are quick to rely on money, impressive buildings and capable staff members, but these have no power in themselves. Nor do the techniques that come in and out of fashion, and on which we place so much emphasis: church growth principles, cell churches, seeker services or planting. They have their place but at their best they are simply vehicles for the communication of the message that is God's power: the cross of Christ.

The message of the cross is not what the world is asking for: 'Jews demand signs and Greeks look for wisdom' (1:22). Still today there are many who expect God to prove his existence by a supernatural display, like the man who shouted at me when I was preaching in the open air, 'Prove God; you can't, can you?' Others look for a version of Christianity that satisfies them intellectually and fits with the world's current mindset, and there are plenty of professing Christians who are prepared to give them what they want. The result is an emasculated gospel, robbed of anything that might cause offence. It is soft on sin and judgment, strong on affirmation, without any call for repentance ('God loves you just as you are – you're wonderful!'), and explicitly denies the uniqueness of Christ, who is offered as just one of many paths up the mountain to God. This new gospel, which really is no gospel at all, may be popular, especially when attractively packaged, but it has no spiritual power. If we want to see people saved from God's wrath and reconciled to him, we must resist the temptation to give people what they want and instead follow Paul's example: 'We preach Christ crucified: a stumbling block to Jews and foolishness to Gentiles, but to those whom God has called, both Jews and Greeks, Christ the power of God and the wisdom of God. For the foolishness of God is wiser than human wisdom, and the weakness of God is stronger than human strength' (1:23–25).

The weakness of preaching . . . and its power

If we want to be spiritually powerful, making an impact on the world as individuals and churches, we must be willing to be weak. God's power works through weak people proclaiming a seemingly weak message, which is often dismissed and despised by the world. Hudson Taylor, the great nineteenth-century missionary to China, was right when he said, 'All God's giants have been weak people.' That is the result of God's deliberate strategy: 'God chose the foolish things of the world to shame the wise; God chose the weak things of the world to shame the strong' (1:27). If he had decided to save people by depending on the brilliant intellect and oratory of especially able preachers, they would receive much of the credit, but as it is, 'No one may boast before him' (1:29), and all the glory goes to God.

When Paul first visited Corinth, he knew that he would be far more acceptable if he gave people the human wisdom they wanted: the kind of teaching they were used to, with a Christian veneer, attractively presented in impressive oratory. However, he deliberately resisted that temptation: 'When I came to you, I did not come with eloquence or human wisdom as I proclaimed to you the testimony about God. For I resolved to know nothing while I was with you except Jesus Christ and him crucified' (2:1–2).

It is no surprise that Paul entered the city 'with much trembling' because the world hates the message of the cross, dismissing it as weak and foolish. And yet, God worked mightily through him and many were converted: 'My message and my preaching were not with wise and persuasive words, but with a demonstration of the Spirit's power, so that your faith might not rest on human wisdom, but on God's power' (2:4–5).

The apostle is hoping that this reminder of the remarkable story of the establishment of their church will awaken the

Corinthians from their spiritual amnesia and prompt them to return to the message through which they were converted. That is a challenge needed by every generation of believers. The devil will always do everything he can to divert the church from the cross. We can hear his voice whenever we are encouraged to believe those scholars who caricature the glorious doctrine of Christ dying in our place to take our punishment as primitive and unbiblical. And we should recognize his evil scheming behind every temptation to sideline the message of Christ crucified and rely instead on human personalities, wisdom, techniques or oratory to make an impact on the world. Let us never forget that true power is found in the weakness of the cross.

2. True wisdom is received by revelation (2:6–16)

The wisdom of the cross

The world may dismiss the gospel of the cross of Christ as foolish, but Paul insists that his message is in fact wise: 'We do, however, speak a message of wisdom among the mature' (2:6). His words contain an implicit rebuke to the Corinthians: if they really were spiritually mature, as they claimed, they would recognize the wisdom of the gospel, but worldly people like them are unable to see it. The cross is God's 'wisdom, a mystery that has been hidden' (2:7), which cannot be discovered or understood by human brain power alone.

Living in an intellectual centre like Oxford, I am bound to acknowledge that human wisdom has achieved much. It was here in 1662 that Robert Boyle devised his law of gas expansion that gave birth to the age of steam, and in 1785 that Edmund Cartwright invented the power loom, which launched the Industrial Revolution. Who knows what achievements may follow in the future – a cure for AIDS or cancer, perhaps? But despite its fine record and the brilliance of the minds gathered in my home city, there is one discovery which Oxford will never be able to boast: the truth about God. The world in its wisdom has split the atom, put men on the moon and created artificial intelligence, but it cannot tell us what God is like or how we can know him.

The Spirit reveals God's wisdom

I was once in a taxi in Indonesia with a friend, when we noticed a hideous object dangling from the mirror. When the driver told us it was his god, my friend asked him if his god spoke to him. The driver just laughed at what was obviously a ridiculous idea; but we were then able to tell him that our God speaks to us. In his amazing grace, God has not left us in the dark but has chosen to reveal his secret wisdom to us by his Spirit: '"What no eye has seen, what no ear has heard, and what no mind has conceived" – the things God has prepared for those who love him – these are the things God has revealed to us by his Spirit' (2:9–10).

In the remarkable verses that follow, Paul describes four stages in the process of the Spirit's revelation of God's wisdom to us:

a) The Spirit knows ('internal revelation')

The Spirit searches all things, even the deep things of God. For who among men knows the thoughts of a man except the man's spirit within him? In the same way no one knows the thoughts of God except the Spirit of God (2:10b–11).

If I concentrate on a particular image in my mind and then ask you to tell me what I am thinking about, the best you can do is guess. You do not know my thoughts, but my spirit, the inner me, does. You would never have suggested that I was imagining an elephant balancing on a tennis ball with a crown on its head, but my spirit shares that knowledge with me.

In a similar way, no-one knows the Father's thoughts except the Spirit. We may call this 'internal revelation'. God himself knows what he is thinking; his word is understood by his Spirit.

b) The Spirit reveals (apostolic revelation)

> *What we have received is not the spirit of the world, but the Spirit who is from God, so that we may understand what God has freely given us* (2:12).

The Spirit does not keep his knowledge of God's wisdom to himself, but reveals it to those Paul refers to as 'we'. It is true that all Christians receive God's Spirit and are therefore able to understand his word, but the context here suggests that Paul is referring chiefly to himself and his fellow apostles, who first received the revelation of the gospel. He seems to use 'I' and 'we' interchangeably in this section, referring to himself in the first person singular in 2:1–5, switching to the plural 'we' in 2:6–16 and then reverting to 'I' in 3:1. He is making a bold personal claim: that the message he and the other apostles received was not invented by them but was rather revealed by the Spirit. Paul is not a religious genius; he is a recipient of divine revelation.

c) The Spirit inspires (scriptural revelation)

> *This is what we speak, not in words taught us by human wisdom but in words taught by the Spirit, expressing spiritual realities with Spirit-taught words* (2:13).

Paul did not keep his God-given knowledge of the gospel to himself, but rather passed it on to others. As he did so, the Spirit who entrusted him with the message also ensured that he passed it on accurately, giving him the very words to say. That is why we can trust the New Testament, confident that it is not simply a human book, but that God spoke through those who wrote it, ensuring that they said exactly what he wanted them to say. The Holy Spirit is the divine author of the Bible and so, if we wish to live by the Spirit, we must listen to its message. We should certainly resist the kind of talk I have sometimes heard: 'I know the Bible teaches X, but I believe the Spirit is telling us Y.' That must be wrong because the Holy Spirit inspired the Bible and will not contradict himself. The voice of the Spirit is found in the teaching of Scripture.

d) The Spirit illumines (individual revelation)

> *The person without the Spirit does not accept the things that come from the Spirit of God but considers them foolishness, and cannot understand them because they are discerned only through the Spirit* (2:14).

Since the fall, when Adam and Eve rebelled against God, human nature has been corrupted so that we are by nature worldly in our thinking. We are unable to understand God's wisdom but rather dismiss it as foolish nonsense. However, 'the spiritual man', the Christian who has received God's Holy Spirit, 'makes judgments about all things' (2:15). The word 'judgments' comes from the same root as the word translated 'discerned' in the previous verse. While the natural man, without the Spirit, has no spiritual discernment and cannot understand or accept God's truth, the Christian is able to see things clearly. For 'who has known the mind of the Lord so as to instruct him?' (2:16). Paul expects us to reply, 'No-one.'

None of us by nature knows God's thoughts. 'But,' he continues, 'we have the mind of Christ' (2:16). By the miracle of
new birth, light has flooded into our dark minds, so that all
who belong to Christ can see things from his perspective. As
a result of our conversion, we no longer find the Bible a dead
book; it has come alive. We can now recognize the message
of the cross for what it is: God's power and wisdom.

This whole passage is designed to correct the Corinthians'
false view of spirituality. They thought they were mature and
spiritual, possibly because they believed they had received a
new revelation from the Spirit that had raised them to an élite
spiritual plane, above Paul and other ordinary Christians
whom they judged inferior. Paul responds by insisting that the
truly spiritual person has not received some extra revelation,
but is rather the Christian who has been enabled to understand and accept God's wisdom: the message of Christ
crucified revealed by the Spirit to the apostles and now found
in the Bible.

It is very important that we grasp this truth. There is no
deeper revelation of the Spirit beyond the revelation of the
Bible. The authentic work of the Spirit is seen, not when
people get excited by some new message or miracle, but
rather when their eyes are opened and their hearts filled with
an ever-deepening appreciation of the Bible's teaching about
what God has done for them in Christ and a growing longing
to live in the light of all they have received from him.

Paul's teaching in these first two chapters of 1 Corinthians
contains important challenges for us today:

- Expect to be considered foolish.
- Don't look for short cuts to spiritual power.
- Never divide the Spirit and the word.
- Always keep the focus on Christ crucified.

Expect to be considered foolish

In *The God Delusion*, Richard Dawkins dismisses the message of the cross as 'vicious, sado-masochistic and repellent'. He continues, 'We should also dismiss it as barking mad, but for its ubiquitous familiarity which has dulled our objectivity. If God wanted to forgive our sins, why not just forgive them, without having himself tortured and executed in payment?'[2] That is a particularly strong expression of a widely held view. The world cannot understand the message of the cross and rejects it as foolish nonsense. We should not be surprised, therefore, if we ourselves are regarded with a mixture of confusion and contempt for holding to the gospel of Christ crucified and trying to explain it to others.

When I announced that I was no longer going to pursue a legal career but would become a pastor instead, one family friend reacted with horror. 'That is the end!' she shouted. It made no sense to her that I should give up the possibility of a job with high status and pay to preach the Christian message. 'What a waste!' She could see the value of a legal career, but what was the use of being a preacher?

It is always hard when family members, colleagues or friends cannot understand why we are so gripped by the gospel. They think we have lost our minds and even been taken in by a cult. The result can be a painful sense of loneliness and disconnection from those around us. Although that is hard, it should be expected. The wisdom of this world, corrupted by the fall, will always regard the cross as weak and foolish. We only recognize its power and wisdom because of the miraculous work of God's Spirit in opening our eyes to understand the truth. Until that miracle occurs in the lives of others, we should expect them to be mystified by us and even contemptuous. Surely this should be a spur to us to pray that God would have mercy on them and enable them to see for themselves the wonder of the cross.

Don't look for short cuts to spiritual power

My pride bristles when I sense that I am being considered weak or foolish because of my Christian faith. The immediate temptation is to prove the other person wrong by trying to impress them in worldly ways. I might talk about the large numbers who come to our church, the size of the staff team or the new congregations we have planted and buildings we have bought, hoping they will be struck by how successful we are. Or I might use clever arguments and show off how much I have read, so that they will know that I am intelligent and knowledgeable. But even if I achieve my goal and they are impressed by my personality and abilities, they are no more likely to become Christians. The power does not lie in myself and anything I am, have or do. Only God can achieve the miracle of conversion as, by his Spirit, he opens blind eyes to see the glories of the crucified and risen Christ.

We would be wrong to take this principle to an extreme and conclude, for example, that it leaves little or no room for apologetics (the use of reasoning to argue for the validity of the Christian faith). Luke explicitly tells us that Paul himself 'reasoned in the synagogue' when he visited Corinth, 'trying to persuade Jews and Greeks' of the truth of the gospel (Acts 18:4). There will be many circumstances in which wise evangelism demands the use of rational argument.

We will meet some people who are convinced that Christianity cannot be true because, for example, they believe there is a contradiction between science and faith, or that the New Testament is not historically reliable. Others are so content with their own world-view that they will not be willing to consider the Christian alternative unless we chip away at their certainties. Even those who are prepared to hear the Christian message may raise objections that cannot just be ignored. Faithful evangelism does not mean simply repeating a formulaic presentation of the ABC of the gospel. We have to use our minds so we can engage intelligently with alternatives to Christianity and objections to it but, as we do so, we must not forget that we will not convert anyone through the brilliance of our arguments. Apologetics should never be an end in itself, but rather a tool that is prayerfully and humbly employed as a means of bringing people to the message of Christ crucified. Conversion is achieved not by intellectual persuasion, but rather by the miraculous power of the Spirit, enabling sinners to believe the gospel.

Never divide the Spirit and the word

It is common to hear of Christians dividing the word and the Spirit, and saying, for example, 'St X's church is strong on the Spirit, but St Y's is strong on the word.' However, the Bible does not allow us to separate the word and the Spirit in that way. If a church is led by the Spirit, it will surely be committed to learning from the Bible, which is inspired by the Spirit; and if it is serious about the Bible, it must also long to live by the Spirit, to whom God's word points so clearly.

The Corinthians claimed to be spiritual, but had drifted from Christ crucified, so Paul directs them back to the message of Scripture. His words in 2:14 would have hurt those who prided themselves on how spiritual they were: 'The man without the Spirit does not accept the things that come from the Spirit of God, for they are foolishness to him, and he cannot understand them, because they are spiritually discerned.' The implication is clear. The apostle is saying, 'If you can't accept the message of God's revelation in Scripture about Christ crucified, which is God's wisdom, that suggests you do not have the Spirit at all, as it is only by the Spirit that we can receive that message.'

Truly spiritual people do not abandon or contradict the teaching of the Bible, but rather make every effort to hear and obey its message. If you want to find a Spirit-filled church, look for one which takes the Bible very seriously and gives time to hearing God speak through it. That will be a church where the sermon is central to its meeting and not a platform for the preachers to put forward their own ideas, but rather a faithful exposition of the truth of Scripture.

Some professing Christians claim that the Bible is out of date and so they adopt new understandings of God's will. As a result, they feel free to reject the clear teaching of the Bible whenever it clashes with the dominant views of our culture, for example, with regard to sexual immorality or the unique-ness of Christ. They may claim that God's Spirit has led them to their reinterpretation of the faith, but Paul's teaching in 1 Corinthians is against them. We are not free to produce our own individual contemporary versions of Christianity; true spirituality recognizes the revelation of God communicated by the Spirit through the apostles in the Bible and seeks to submit to it.

It is not just those who overtly put Scripture aside who can lead us from the paths of true spirituality. We should also be wary of the danger posed by those who may uphold the Bible's teaching in theory and yet in practice preach a very different message. We should not be dazzled by the brilliance of preachers, their popularity, the miracles they may claim to have performed or the number of people who speak of the spiritual benefit they have received from their ministry. Paul's teaching in 1 Corinthians 1 – 2 urges us to keep a clear head and ask of any church or leader: Is their aim to sit under the teaching of the Bible and proclaim what it says, rather than dismiss and distort it? And does their message focus on the Lord Jesus Christ and his cross? If not, it comes from human wisdom, not God's; it is worldliness, not true spirituality.

Always keep the focus on Christ crucified

Paul's resolution as he entered Corinth 'to know nothing . . . except Jesus Christ and him crucified' (2:2) presents a challenging example for us. We must not take his words as a justification for a wooden form of evangelism which makes no real attempt to engage with people or listen to them, but just recites the same few basic truths at every opportunity. It is very clear from Luke's account of his missionary journeys in Acts, and from his own letters, that Paul sought to teach people 'the whole will of God' (Acts 20:27) when he taught them the gospel and presented it in a variety of ways, depending on his audience. We should not, therefore, understand him to be saying in 1 Corinthians 2:2 that he only ever spoke about the cross of Christ when he was in Corinth and not, for example, his incarnation, resurrection, ascension or return as well. In fact, later on he explicitly states that the resurrection was central to his message (15:3–4). Paul's declaration should be taken rather as an expression of his determination never to be deflected from the central importance of the cross in his life and preaching, despite its unpopularity in the world. We too should make the same resolution.

I vividly remember the first time the Holy Spirit opened my eyes to understand the amazing truth that Christ had died for me. Until then God had been a rather distant figure who left me cold, but now I knew that he was my Father who loved me so much that he had sent his only Son to die for me. Such love blew my mind and softened my heart to love God like I had never done before. It is always challenging to remember those early days after my conversion and ask myself if I am still as thrilled by the message of the cross as I was then.

Of course, it is right to seek to grow in understanding of the depth and breadth of the Bible's teaching, but that growth must always spring from the foundation of the message of Christ crucified. If some new teaching or movement, which claims to be from the Spirit, has led me to shift my focus away from the crucified Christ, I should be concerned. The Holy Spirit will keep pointing me back to the cross, enabling me to delight in it myself, as well as prompting me to point others to it. We should pray that the Holy Spirit would enable us to keep proclaiming the praises of the crucified Christ all our days on earth until we join the chorus of heaven: 'Worthy is the Lamb, who was slain' (Revelation 5:12).

Bible study (1 Corinthians 1 – 2)

1. In what circumstances are you made to feel weak and foolish as Christians by the unbelieving world?
2. Read through 1 Corinthians 1 – 2. Which words and themes are repeated?

1:17–31

3. What does Paul mean by 'the wisdom of the world' (1:20)? What are its limitations?
4. What do you learn about true spiritual power and wisdom?
5. Do people still seek 'signs' and 'wisdom' (1:22)? In what ways are you tempted to give them what they want?

2:1–5

6. What did it mean for Paul 'to know nothing . . . except Jesus Christ and him crucified' (2:2) when he visited Corinth?
7. What will the same attitude mean for us today?

2:6–16

8. How does God reveal his wisdom to us?
9. What is the relationship between the Spirit and the Bible?
10. What are the practical implications of these truths for us?

Finally . . .

11. What have you learnt about true spirituality from these chapters?
12. What alternative thinking does this challenge?

2. TRUE SPIRITUALITY respects faithful leaders, not flashy ones

(1 Corinthians 3 – 4)

How do you spot a Christian leader?

It had been a good wedding, and I was enjoying myself at the reception. I was placed on a table with a group of people I had not met before, and we were getting on well, but then came the question: 'Tell me, Vaughan, what do you do?' Some ministerial friends of mine have developed brilliant answers to such questions that open up great evangelistic opportunities, but they always sound pretentious when I use them, so I simply said, 'I'm a Christian pastor.' The shock wave that went round my new companions was almost visible as, no doubt, they replayed the previous half-hour's conversation in their minds, trying to remember if they had said anything unsuitable for my clerical ears. Then, after a few seconds' silence, the man on my right said, 'I'd never have known; you don't fit my idea of a minister at all.' When I asked him what he would expect me to be like, he described an older man wearing black clothes and a sombre expression.

How do you spot a Christian leader? It is vital that we are able to answer that question, not so that we can avoid social embarrassment, but, far more importantly, so we know who we can trust to teach and guide us as Christians. It is possible for some to have the title 'Reverend' or 'Pastor', and yet not be exercising a truly Christian ministry. How can we distinguish between the fake and the genuine, the worldly and the spiritual? Our leaders have a huge influence over us, for good or ill, so we urgently need wisdom in this area. Wrong decisions about which leaders we will follow and which preachers we will listen to cause more believers to wander from the paths of true spirituality than perhaps any other issue today. That certainly was the case in Corinth, where believers' decisions in this area were one more manifestation of their foolish immaturity. Paul's correction of their worldly thinking about leaders has much to say to us.

'Why don't you treat us like adults?'

'Why don't you treat me like an adult?' complains the teenager. She is convinced of her own maturity: she wears adult clothes, listens to adult music and has a Saturday job, yet her parents insist on treating her as if she were still a child. She is never allowed out on her own, has to ring home as soon as she arrives anywhere and must always return by ten o'clock at night. It is almost too much for her to bear. 'Why don't you treat me like an adult?' she cries indignantly. Her parents reply, as parents always do: 'We'll treat you like an adult when you start behaving like an adult. Only yesterday you pulled your little brother's hair and kicked over his Lego castle; is that adult behaviour? And, when we last let you go somewhere on your own, you got the wrong bus and ended up on the other side of the city with no money, so we had to go all that way to collect you. How can we give you more freedom when you still need looking after like a child?'

Paul begins chapter 3 by speaking to the Corinthians with similar language. They were proud of their spiritual maturity, no doubt pointing to their spiritual gifts as evidence: they spoke in tongues, prophesied and healed, and yet, to their great frustration, Paul, their spiritual father who had first led them to Christ, still treated them like children. His gospel, which focused on Christ and his cross, was all very well when they were spiritual babies, but they could not stick with it now that they had grown up as Christians. That would be like a twenty-year-old still watching *Teletubbies* or *Sesame Street* on television. They had moved on to a more adult message provided for them by the new leaders in Corinth, who had emerged after Paul had left. Some even wondered what they had ever seen in the apostle. He was weak and unimpressive compared to their new spiritual heroes, and could not even preach very well, not using any of the rhetorical techniques in vogue at the time. They could have borne his inadequacies more easily if only he would face facts and recognize that they were not spiritual babies any more: 'Why don't you treat us like adults, Paul?'

Personality cults

Paul replies to their complaints at the beginning of chapter 3 with words that were devastating for a church that prided itself on its mature spirituality: 'Brothers, I could not address you as spiritual but as worldly – mere infants in Christ' (3:1). As proof of their immature worldliness, he points to the factionalism of the church, which he has already referred to in 1:12: 'You are still worldly. For since there is jealousy and quarrelling among you, are you not worldly? Are you not acting like mere men? For when one says, "I follow Paul," and another, "I follow Apollos," are you not mere men?' (3:3–4). Far from being led by the Holy Spirit, as they claimed, their behaviour showed that they were taking their cue from the non-Christian world around them.

We might expect hero worship from teenagers, but it is pathetic to see a sixty-year-old who has not grown out of it and still has Elvis posters plastered all over the house. The Corinthians were like that: elderly groupies, still fanatically loyal to their particular Christian hero. Paul says to them, 'Such behaviour is childish; you need to grow up as Christians.'

Twenty-first-century Christians are often just the same. We copy the world in its obsession with personalities, dividing into parties which gather around different Christian gurus whose teaching is exalted almost to the level of infallibility. Those who attach themselves to other leaders can be seen as enemies, even though they are fellow Christians who believe exactly the same as us on all the fundamentals of the faith and worship the same Heavenly Father. Sadly, membership of the same Christian family can be seen as less important than membership of the same faction. Sometimes the leader is to blame for promoting such adulation by drawing attention to himself and encouraging an unquestioning loyalty from his followers; but often leaders placed on pedestals are as uneasy as the apostle was when people said, 'I follow Paul.' He was horrified at the thought of Christians gathering around him rather than around the Lord he served. To counter their immature, worldly thinking, he outlines a truly spiritual understanding of Christian leadership that never allows mere humans to take centre stage. Churches should value not those who are the most flashy, with impressive gifts and personalities, but rather those who are faithful in fulfilling their charge, and point to their master, not themselves. Paul stresses that faithful Christian leaders are:

1. servants who preach the cross (3:5 – 4:7)
2. fools who live the cross (4:8–21).

1. Servants who preach the cross (3:5 - 4:7)

Servants of God

There is no evidence of any tension between Paul, who planted the church in Corinth, and Apollos, who led it after the apostle had left, yet both had their supporters and opponents. There were still some who remained loyal to Paul, thinking he could do no wrong, while others preferred his successor, and these preferences had developed into an unseemly rivalry with an unhealthy focus on the leaders. Paul responds by drawing the Corinthians' attention back to God: 'What, after all, is Apollos? And what is Paul? Only servants, through whom you came to believe – as the Lord has assigned to each his task' (3:5). The message for the twenty-first century will hit home if we substitute the names of the spiritual leaders we most admire today for those of Apollos and Paul. The apostle uses an illustration from horticulture to underline his point: 'I planted the seed, Apollos watered it, but God made it grow' (3:6).

When I was at primary school, our teacher gave the class some tiny seeds and instructed us to place them on soggy paper at the bottom of a pot. 'Just watch,' she said, 'and in a few days it will be full of cress.' I was sceptical, but it was not long before the miracle occurred. It was very hard for me to take any credit for the crop of cress I was able to put in my sandwiches for a day or two. All I had done was add water to a few seeds; God did the rest. Paul explains it is just the same when people come to faith in Christ or grow as believers: human beings have a part to play in sharing the gospel message with others and making disciples of them, but only God can produce the miracle of faith and transformation in those who hear. 'So,' Paul tells us, 'neither he who plants nor he who waters is anything, but only God, who makes things grow' (3:7).

That is a vital lesson for us to learn, not just so we are able to share God's view of other Christian leaders, but also so that we maintain a proper humility ourselves. We can feel very important and allow our chests to swell when we are given responsibilities in our churches. That certainly happened to me when I was asked to be the president of my university Christian Union. A few weeks later, I went to help on a summer camp for teenagers, fully expecting that I would have an important role that suited my new status, but in fact my chief responsibility was to maintain the stock of toilet rolls around the site. Perhaps the leaders sensed I was a bit full of myself and needed a reminder of the true nature of leadership; if so, it was exactly what I needed: Christian leaders are just servants of God.

Mark Ruston, Vicar of the Round Church in Cambridge for over thirty years, was a great example of a humble Christian servant. As a result of his faithful preaching and personal ministry to generations of students and townsfolk, large numbers came to faith and were led into full-time gospel ministry. On his retirement, many of us gathered to thank him for his godly example and the impact his ministry had had on us. As speaker after speaker stood to pay tribute to his many qualities, Mark visibly squirmed in his seat. At last he had his turn to reply: 'If a neighbour lends you a donkey to do a job for you, you may give it some straw for its pains, and I thank you for the straw you have given me,' he said, pointing to the television he had just received as a present, 'but above all, you don't thank the donkey, you thank the master who has loaned him to you.' He then closed with a prayer of thanksgiving to God, having first invited us to sing:

How good is the God we adore!
Our faithful, unchangeable friend:
His love is as great as his power
and knows neither measure nor end.

For Christ is the first and the last;
His Spirit will guide us safe home:
we'll praise him for all that is past
and trust him for all that's to come.[1]

Mark's attitude was just what Paul longed to see in the Corinthians. If only they would keep their attention focused on God, they would repent of their hero worship of their leaders and the divisive attitude that flowed from it. After all, if every Christian worker who proclaims the gospel of Christ is his servant, it follows that they are all on the same side. They may have different roles, but they are used by the same master to serve the same end: to bring in a good harvest. That means that if some other leader, whom we have pitted against our spiritual hero, is involved in gospel ministry, he is not an enemy. We may not agree with absolutely everything he says or does, but, if he is faithfully proclaiming Christ and his cross, he too is a servant of the same master. 'The man who plants and the man who waters have one purpose' (3:8); they are 'God's fellow-workers', and the church is 'God's field, God's building' (3:9). We do not belong to Pastor Bloggs' church or the Reverend Buggins' party; they are just God's servants and we are God's people.

Judged by God

The Corinthians were not just worldly and immature in the way they overexalted their leaders, but also in the way they appraised their work. They judged their new leaders very favourably, whereas they looked down on Paul, who persisted in focusing on the message of Christ and his cross, which they associated with their spiritual infancy. The new generation of Christian leaders in Corinth treated them like adults and proclaimed a much more sophisticated message. Its power was obvious from the leaders' popularity. No doubt their churches were packed; they were invited to speak at crowded conventions and their books sold like hotcakes; perhaps the secular press had even begun to take an interest in them. Paul, by contrast, was scorned and derided by almost everyone, inside and outside the church. As far as most of the Corinthians were concerned, there was no contest: Paul had been tried and found wanting. But Paul was not concerned about their judgment; what mattered to him was the verdict of a much higher court. The Corinthians showed their spiritual immaturity by judging according to worldly standards, so Paul pointed them to the very different and far more important judgment of God.

Paul switches his metaphor in verses 10–15 from a field to a building: he laid the foundation (3:10) and now other leaders are building on it. Perhaps superficially they were doing a great job: the church was known far and wide as a successful, growing one, but the apostle warns them not to be taken in by appearances. However impressive a church may look, only God's judgment at the end of time will reveal its true quality. Only then will it be clear if its leaders have deserved the praise they received on earth, or whether they were guilty of shoddy workmanship. In Paul's words: 'If any man builds on this foundation using gold, silver, costly stones, wood, hay or straw, his work will be shown for what it is, because the Day will bring it to light. It will be revealed with fire, and the fire will test the quality of each man's work' (3:12–13).

The inadequacy of superficial judgments

I received a humbling lesson in the importance of not relying too much on premature, superficial judgments during my time as a student. The highlight of the university's charity 'rag week' was a sponsored bed race with the teams fiercely competing with one another in trying to propel a bed around the town as quickly as possible; cars were kept off the streets for the occasion, and crowds turned up to cheer their support. My team was secretly confident of victory, having spent hours putting oil on all the right places and decorating our bed with an elaborate design. There was no doubt that it was easily the most attractive on display, and the crowd gave it appreciative applause as we reached the starting line. It was hard not to look down smugly at the other beds that were so dilapidated and scruffy by comparison, but there were no prizes for beauty at the start; what mattered was who finished fastest. We began well, but it was not long before our beautiful bed began to disintegrate, as one wheel and then another fell off, so that we were forced to suffer the indignity of picking up the pieces and dragging it off the road at least a mile before the end. The warm applause before the start counted for nothing; we had failed in the one judgment that really mattered – the race itself.

The superficial judgment of the Corinthians may have concluded that the new teachers were far superior to Paul, but he points them to the future judgment of God, which will reveal the true quality of any Christian leader's work. Some will be rewarded; their teaching has been fruitful, and so the fruit of their ministry lasts (3:14). Many from their churches will join them in eternity, and they will be welcomed into

God's presence with the wonderful words of Jesus: 'Well done, good and faithful servant!' (Matthew 25:21).

There will be others, however, who have not been faithful to Christ and his teaching, and will therefore suffer shame on that day. Maybe they pointed to themselves and not to Christ, so that within their church or youth group they created personal disciples, dependent on them, rather than men and women of faith, trusting in Christ. Or perhaps they tried to give people the message they wanted to hear, rather than faithfully proclaiming God's word from the Bible, even when it was unpopular and went against the grain of the culture. As a result, much of their work does not last. The church, youth ministry or Sunday school they led may have looked impressive, but if its growth was produced by something other than the faithful preaching of the message of Christ and his cross, it will not survive the day of judgment, for it is 'wood, hay or straw' (1 Corinthians 3:12), and will be consumed in the fire. If they belong to Christ, they will still be with him in eternity, but there will be no fanfare or warm congratulations on their arrival. They must suffer an undignified entrance into heaven, 'as one escaping through the flames' (3:15), like a man leaping from a burning building just before it collapses. Others will not be as fortunate: if their teaching was so full of falsehood that it led to the total spiritual destruction of those whom they were supposed to pastor, they can expect no mercy from God. The Christian church is God's precious temple that he loves deeply and where he has chosen to live. Paul therefore issues this solemn warning: 'If anyone destroys God's temple, God will destroy him' (3:17).

Stewards of God

We want our leaders to be impressive, with big personalities, winsome charm, great learning and a natural eloquence – the kind of people we can introduce to our non-Christian friends without fear of embarrassment. Our friends might not agree with their message, but at least they cannot deny their abilities. However, although those outward qualities might be useful, they are certainly not of central importance. Paul insists that what God is looking for above all in Christian leaders is, not flashiness, but faithfulness.

The Corinthians had grown tired of Paul with his rather dull delivery and focus on the cross of Christ, which was such an embarrassment in sophisticated Corinth. They much preferred the new leaders with their elegant turns of phrase, brilliant rhetorical flourishes and clever ideas, but they had been judging according to the wrong criteria. They had failed to remember that Christian leaders are not ultimately accountable to any individual or church, but to God. They are 'servants of Christ' who have been 'entrusted with the secret things of God' (4:1). This is the language of stewardship.

'The secret things' are the great truths of the gospel, with its focus on the cross of Christ, which Paul has earlier described as 'God's secret wisdom' (2:7). As stewards of Christ, Christian leaders have the awesome responsibility and privilege of proclaiming the message of the gospel to others. When they stand before their master on judgment day, they will not be judged according to their natural abilities, but rather according to how faithfully they have discharged the tasks that were given to them, for, as Paul puts it, 'it is required that those who have been given a trust must prove faithful' (4:2). The questions put to leaders on that day will not be 'Were you a brilliant communicator who could hold an audience spellbound with your jokes and heartrending stories?', 'Did you lead an impressive church full of hundreds of people?' or 'Did you gain a good reputation in the world for your learning and oratory?' God's questions will rather be 'Were you faithful?',

'Did you fulfil the tasks entrusted to you?', 'Did you hold faithfully to the gospel of Christ crucified proclaimed in the Scriptures?' and 'Did you persevere in seeking to live by that gospel and to preach it to others?'

2. Fools who live the cross (4:8–21)

Fools for Christ

Joseph Parker, Minister of the City Temple in London at the end of the nineteenth century, was entering his pulpit when a woman in the gallery threw a piece of paper at him. He bent down to pick it up and saw just one word: 'FOOL!' He then began his sermon with the words, 'I have received many anonymous letters in my time – texts without a signature, but today for the first time I have received a signature without a text!'[2]

It is not flattering to be described as a fool, and yet that was a title that Paul actually used of himself and his fellow apostles, saying, 'We are fools for Christ' (4:10). He made that claim to counter the Corinthians' false impression of what leaders blessed by God looked like. No doubt they imagined powerful, impressive Titans who towered above the problems that lesser mortals encountered and sailed through life enjoying great victories – the spiritual equivalent of James Bond. But Paul certainly did not fit that description: he faced great suffering and it did not bounce off him; he was deeply affected – shaken and stirred.

To make his point, Paul uses a series of dramatic metaphors. He begins by taking us to the amphitheatre where we can imagine the arena packed with excited holiday crowds. The games would begin with a procession into the stadium, led by distinguished VIPs at the front, but Paul tells the Corinthians to look for the apostles not among them, but rather among the pathetic, despised criminals who trailed in at the back. He says, 'God has put us apostles on display at the end of the procession, like men condemned to die in the arena' (4:9). They were alongside those who would provide the grand finale to the day's entertainment by being forced to fight with gladiators or thrown to the lions.

The scum of the earth

Paul then takes us out of the amphitheatre into the kitchen. 'Up to this moment,' he writes, 'we have become the scum of the earth, the refuse of the world' (4:13). The words 'scum' and 'refuse' are virtually synonymous, referring to the filth that is removed in the process of cleaning. Paul might point us to a pile of dust, with bits of onion peel and mouldy crumbs of bread, that has just been swept up on the floor, or to the gunge in the plughole after some filthy pans have been washed up. 'That's what we're like,' he is saying. As people turn their noses up in disgust at rubbish in the kitchen, so they despise Paul and the other apostles.

The contrast with how the Corinthians viewed themselves could not have been greater. Paul writes with heavy irony, 'Already you have all you want! Already you have become rich! You have become kings – and that without us! How I wish that you really had become kings so that we might be kings with you!' (4:8). It is as if he is saying, 'You Corinthians really are a cut above the rest, aren't you! You've managed to zoom up to heaven and leave us apostles behind!'

These words of Paul take us to the heart of the Corinthian problem: they thought they had arrived spiritually and were already enjoying the fullness of God's salvation. Later in the letter we find that they did not believe there was any future resurrection to look forward to (15:12); in their minds, all the blessings of salvation were available now. They believed they already reigned with Christ and could therefore be free from suffering and struggle, enjoying a powerful, triumphant resurrection life. However, they had got their chronology wrong and were claiming for now what God had only promised in the future. The fullness of salvation can be enjoyed only when Christ returns and introduces a perfect new creation. Until then, we cannot leave the cross behind, and we must not only continue to proclaim its message, but also expect to share its experience: weakness, suffering and derision, which remain very much part of life in this fallen world. As Paul writes, 'To this very hour we go hungry and thirsty, we are in rags, we are brutally treated, we are homeless' (4:11).

That was a lesson the Corinthians urgently needed to learn. Their wrong understanding of their present position resulted in wrong expectations of their leaders. Paul's suffering and rejection convinced them that he could not possibly be a leader anointed by God; but they should have known from the example and words of the master he served that 'God's power is made perfect in weakness' (2 Corinthians 12:9). The Lord Jesus went to glory via the cross and told his disciples to travel the same road. Those who are faithful to him will suffer and can expect to be rejected by many. Authentic Christian workers are not only servants who proclaim the cross, but fools, at least in the eyes of the world, who live the cross.

Paul's teaching about leadership in 1 Corinthians 3 – 4 contains much-needed warnings for us today:

- Faithfulness matters more than success.
- Don't undervalue the faithful plodder.
- Don't put pastors on pedestals.
- Don't bypass the way of the cross.

Faithfulness matters more than success

Kent Hughes served for many years as the much-loved pastor of College Church in Wheaton, Illinois, from where his preaching ministry has had a global impact, not least through his writing. In the book, *Liberating Ministry from the Success Syndrome*, co-written with his wife Barbara, he reflected on his early days as an unknown pastor when planting a new church out of a large and thriving congregation. He had spent months preparing: praying, getting to know the target area and gathering a gifted core team. Everything was in place and everyone assumed that the new church would grow rapidly, but it did not. In fact, after six months of punishing hard work, the attendance was lower than at the start. As a result, Kent sank into the deepest depression of his life and considered giving up. But that dark period was used by God to expose an unbiblical pattern in his thinking.

The turning point was when he began to distinguish between worldly understandings of success and God's perspective. He writes, 'It was a banner day in our lives when we saw from the Bible that great public success in the ministry . . . is not necessarily success in God's eyes. *God's call is to be faithful rather than successful.* This brought Barbara and me to a profound and liberating realization. We saw how success was equally possible for those in the most difficult of situations – for example, those with small numbers and inadequate resources – as well as those having vast ministries.'[3] They summed up the lesson they learnt in one simple phrase: 'Success is faithfulness.'[4]

The Hughes had grasped the truth that Paul stresses in 1 Corinthians 3 and 4. He is a failure as far as they are concerned, weak and foolish, but he does not let that affect the focus of his ministry. He can even say, 'I care very little if I am judged by you or by any human court; indeed, I do not even judge myself'

(4:3). It is God's judgment that matters to him (4:4); his chief ambition is to be faithful to his master and fulfil his charge.

Our ministries, whether as pastors or in other roles, would be transformed if we were all to share that same passion, but too often we are driven by the desire to please other people instead. The result is compromise, and often exhaustion, as we desperately try to fulfil the conflicting demands that others lay upon us, and it can be devastating if we still fail to live up to their expectations and find ourselves unpopular. The only escape from that treadmill is the liberation discovered by the Hughes – realizing that what ultimately matters is faithfulness to Jesus Christ.

Don't undervalue the faithful plodder

There is a real danger that what we call spirituality is in fact worldliness. Are we really as clued-up and mature as we think? Or are we still spiritually childish in our thinking? We must not be dazzled by what the world values: big personalities, supernatural phenomena and clever arguments, but rather judge ourselves and our leaders by God's standards, 'For the wisdom of this world is foolishness in God's sight' (3:19). God looks for faithful leaders, not flashy ones.

We too often adopt worldly thinking in our attitude and expect leaders to live up to our impossibly high standards. It is no wonder that so many Christians never settle for long in any church but move from one to the next, looking for the pastor who will live up to their unrealistic dreams. Our expectations not only lead to constant dissatisfaction in us, but also place enormous pressure on leaders. Many think that they cannot admit to any weakness, for fear of being rejected. Others struggle with a constant feeling of inadequacy as they sense the congregation's frustration that they are not as able as the preachers they listen to online.

Of course, natural abilities are given by God and can be used by him, but they are far less important than obedience to Christ's commission. It is much better to sit under the ministry of a faithful plodder with average gifts, who is diligently living and teaching the true message of the Bible, than to attend a church led by a ten-talent star who relies on his own brilliance rather than on the power of God's word. Very few pastors have exceptional abilities. Most of those God uses are ordinary people entrusted with an extra-ordinary gospel. Their task is simply to do their best with the personalities and gifts they have been given; God will do the rest. So when we are next frustrated with our leader's failings, let us resist the temptation to complain and pray instead.

Don't put pastors on pedestals

While our worldly attitude towards leaders can lead to excessive criticism on the one hand, it can also result in idoliz-ation on the other. That was happening in Corinth where the Christians attached themselves to different leaders and hero-worshipped them in an unhealthy way. Paul insists, however, that our focus must be exclusively on the Father, Son and Holy Spirit. The church is a field in which God the Father causes the growth (3:7); a building of whom God the Son is the foun-dation (3:11); and a temple in which God the Spirit is the inhabitant (3:16). Christians do not belong to any human being, but to God.

God commands us to respect our leaders, but we must resist any tendency to put them on pedestals and place too much focus on them. In our global society, some pastors achieve international celebrity status, speak at conferences around the world and are listened to by millions via the Internet. We can thank God for their gifts and learn from their ministries, but we must never forget that they are simply God's servants: their role is to point beyond themselves to God via his word. Let us make sure we focus on the message and the great God of whom it speaks, not on the messenger.

Don't bypass the way of the cross

Paul wants us to follow his example in being willing to be fools for Christ. Will we embrace the message of the cross, insisting that there is no other way to get right with God, even if such a claim is dismissed as naive or arrogant? And will we embrace the life of the cross, accepting that we are not in heaven yet and that suffering is inevitable for those who are prepared to be faithful to Christ?

Charles Simeon was one man who did imitate Paul. For fifty-four years, from 1782 to 1836, he served as minister of Holy Trinity Church in Cambridge, and for much of that time he was despised, not only by most of the citizens of Cambridge, but also by the long-standing members of his own church. His appointment to the job, as a young man of twenty-three, was very unpopular, and many of the church members boycotted the services and locked the pews to prevent anyone from sitting in them. When Simeon bought chairs and put them in the aisles so that the many students who had begun to attend could sit there, the lay leadership threw the chairs out of the building so that a large proportion of the congregation had to stand. This fierce opposition continued for years, but Simeon never wavered from the faithful proclamation of the gospel. Then the tide slowly turned. By the time of his death, many hundreds had been converted through his ministry, and his grateful congregation placed an epitaph in the church that should be coveted by all gospel ministers:

In Memory of
THE REV. CHARLES SIMEON, M.A.,
Senior Fellow of King's College,
And fifty-four years vicar of this parish; who,
whether as the ground of his own hopes,
or as the subject of all his ministrations,
determined to know nothing but
JESUS CHRIST AND HIM CRUCIFIED.
I Cor.II.2.

Bible study (1 Corinthians 3 - 4)

3:1–4

1. What was it that caused Paul to say that the Corinthians were spiritually childish?
2. How is such behaviour seen in churches today?
3. In what way is your attitude towards Christian leaders unhealthy?

3:5 – 4:7

4. What does Paul teach about:
   - leaders?
   - the church?
5. What are the implications for:
   - how we behave as leaders ourselves?
   - how we respond to the leadership of others?

4:8–21

6. What point is Paul making by contrasting them and the apostle?
7. What are the implications for your expectations in the Christian life?
8. What will it mean for you to 'imitate' Paul (verse 16)?

Finally . . .

9. What have you learnt about true spirituality?
10. What alternative thinking does this challenge?

3. TRUE SPIRITUALITY
demands holiness, not moral permissiveness

(1 Corinthians 5 – 6)

A permissive society

The BBC showed a programme recently called *The Summer of Love, 1967*. This year, we were told, 'was the summer when the young cast off the cloak of convention and threw themselves into social, sexual and pharmacological revolution, which shocked society to its very foundations'. A succession of ageing ex-hippies then appeared on the screen to talk about the Beatles, the pill, mini-skirts and marijuana.

Of course we cannot date its onset so precisely to just one year, but undoubtedly the 1960s did witness a social revolution which led to the 'Permissive Society' with its familiar slogans: 'If it feels good, do it'; 'Whatever turns you on'; and 'Anything goes'. It became popular to think, and even say, 'It is forbidden to forbid.' Many have adopted a similar mindset and refuse to accept any values imposed on them from outside, whether from society, institutions or God. They insist, 'I am free to live my own life as I choose, as long as I am not overtly harming anyone. I can do whatever I want.' This mentality tends to reject 'religion', which is regarded as a relic from the past, as authoritarian, divisive and, according to nearly half of Britons in a recent poll, 'harmful'.[1] However, a vague form of 'spirituality', which makes no uncomfortable claims to objective truth or moral demands, remains popular. In the words of Martin Wroe of *The Observer*, 'The consumer is champion and personal choice is everything . . . This is the era of the do-it-yourself faith, of making your own god.'[2] It is hardly surprising that this kind of spirituality never says 'no', but always affirms us in whatever lifestyle we choose.

A permissive church

We expect to see such a morally permissive attitude in the world, but we should be deeply shocked when it is found overtly in the church, as was the case in Corinth. In fact, in Corinth the church's permissiveness was even greater than that seen in the world. Paul writes, 'It is actually reported that there is sexual immorality among you, and of a kind that does not occur even among pagans' (5:1). This lax attitude towards immorality is another example of the false spirituality of the Corinthian church which, sadly, has much in common with contemporary Christianity.

True spirituality

If we wish to be truly spiritual, we are not simply to seek great experiences of God, but rather to strive to grow in holiness. We are called to become more like Christ as we bear the fruit of the Spirit: 'Love, joy, peace, patience, kindness, goodness, faithfulness, gentleness and self-control' (Galatians 5:22–23). This process of growing in godliness, or 'sanctification', must include a determined effort, once again motivated and empowered by the Spirit, to fight against sin and 'put to death the misdeeds of the body' (Romans 8:13). If we 'live by the Spirit' we 'will not gratify the desires of the sinful nature', such as 'sexual immorality, impurity and debauchery; idolatry and witchcraft; hatred, discord, jealousy, fits of rage, selfish ambition, dissensions, factions and envy; drunkenness, orgies and the like' (Galatians 5:16, 19–21).

This emphasis on the necessity of godly living is urgently needed today, and was certainly needed in a Corinthian church which had been corrupted by a world which, like ours, did not like to say 'no'. From the very start of the letter, Paul stresses the need for the church to be holy and distinct from the world in its behaviour. He describes Christians as those 'sanctified in Christ Jesus and called to be holy' (1 Corinthians 1:2), no doubt making that point early in the letter because the Corinthians placed little, if any, emphasis on the need for holiness. They had a lax attitude to sin, which flowed from their limited view of the spiritual life. As they saw it, spirituality focused on individuals enjoying spiritual experiences in their souls in the here and now. Throughout the letter, Paul corrects them, insisting that true spirituality is not just about oneself, but about all of us; it is not just about the present, but also looks to the future; and it is certainly not just concerned with the soul, but also has significant implications for how we behave with our bodies. True spirituality, he stresses, demands holiness, not moral permissiveness.

In 1 Corinthians 5 – 6 Paul challenges their indifference to immorality and argues that a sinful lifestyle is incompatible with:

1. the health of the church (5:1–13)
2. the realities of the future (6:1–11)
3. the significance of the body (6:12–20).

1. A sinful lifestyle is incompatible with the health of the church

A terrible sin

Paul begins 1 Corinthians 5 by referring to one especially shocking example of their permissiveness: 'A man has his father's wife' (5:1). If this man had been sleeping with his mother, we can assume the apostle would have said so explicitly, so it seems that the sexual relationship was with his stepmother (and the tense indicates an ongoing sinful relationship). Even the pagan Corinthians would not tolerate such behaviour, which was saying something, as Corinth was notorious for its sexual immorality. Paul was outraged by the Corinthian Christians' indifference: 'And you are proud!' he exclaims. He is horrified that such scandalous behaviour does not dent their confidence that they are truly spiritual. It may even be that they are proud of their ability to accommodate such a relationship, and that they see it as an assertion of their Christian liberty – their freedom in Christ to do what they want. Perhaps they used it as evidence to support their boast that they were no longer bound by the shackles of the law or the old taboos, but had been liberated.

Church discipline

Paul says, 'Shouldn't you rather have been filled with grief and have put out of your fellowship the man who did this?' (5:2). Those words begin one of the most significant passages in the New Testament concerning the importance and nature of church discipline. The Reformers in the sixteenth century taught that discipline was one of the essential marks of a true church, but it is very rare today. The lack of such discipline, even in the face of the persistent sin of church leaders, is one of the issues causing great distress among orthodox believers in various denominations. Liberal Christians sometimes respond by quoting the words of Jesus in the Sermon on the Mount: 'Do not judge, or you too will be judged' (Matthew 7:1). There is undoubtedly an important challenge for us all in those words, but they must not be misunderstood. The Lord Jesus is condemning censoriousness: a judgmentalism that flows from a self-righteous superiority that is forever seeing faults in others, but is blind to its own faults. To those guilty of that kind of critical spirit, Jesus says, 'First take the plank out of your own eye, and then you will see clearly to remove the speck from your brother's eye' (Matthew 7:5). That is an important principle, perhaps especially for those of us who are concerned for the purity of the church and call on church leaders to maintain it. However, in condemning judgmentalism, Jesus is not forbidding any kind of judging. A few verses later he warns us to 'watch out for false prophets' (Matthew 7:15), which requires us to make a judgment as to which of those who claim to speak in God's name are true and which are false. And in Matthew 18:15–20 he teaches explicitly on the subject of church discipline.

Jesus makes it clear that church discipline is sometimes necessary, but he stresses that it should take place only as a last resort. He says that, if a Christian brother or sister sins against us, we should go to them privately and show them their faults. The matter should be taken further only if there is no repentance, in which case we should take one or two others to speak to them. Only if there is still no repentance should the case be brought before the whole church, when another opportunity should be given for the individual to repent. Discipline should follow only if, even then, there is no recognition of fault or willingness to turn from sin. Discipline, therefore, is a reluctant and final action after a lengthy process. Paul is certainly not teaching that, if anyone is found guilty of sin, however serious, they should immediately be cast out of the church. The situation in 1 Corinthians 5 is that of an individual persisting in sin after repeated appeals to repent have been rejected. At this stage the church is bound to discipline the sinner.

Church discipline is good for the sinner

Paul called on the church to 'hand this man over to Satan, so that the sinful nature may be destroyed and his spirit saved on the day of the Lord' (5:5). The intention is loving, not vindictive. To 'hand this man over to Satan' is not to send him to hell, but rather to expel him from the church and send him into the world where Satan, who is 'the god of this world', holds sway (2 Corinthians 4:4, ESV). The individual is no longer to be regarded as a member of the church and should certainly not be welcomed as a brother at the Lord's table. The goal is not simply punitive, but is that 'the sinful nature may be destroyed'.

The word translated 'sinful nature' literally means 'flesh'. It could be that Paul means the man's body and envisages that he may get sick and even die as a result of God's judgment. It is true that in 1 Corinthians 11:30 Paul does speak of physical consequences as a result of sin on one particular occasion, but it is perhaps more likely here that by 'flesh', Paul means the fallen part of the man's nature: his 'sinful nature', as in the NIV translation. Paul is hoping that the church's action in casting the sinner out of church will prompt him to come to his senses and repent, so that he refuses to go the way of the sinful nature any more and, as a result, will be ready for the day of judgment (5:5b). So, church discipline is a loving action, designed to have a positive impact on the individual sinner.

Church discipline is good for the church

The Corinthian Christians were selfish and individualistic, as becomes very clear later in the letter by the way they demanded their rights, regardless of the effect on others (1 Corinthians 8 – 10), gorged themselves on food and drink at the Lord's Supper, without a thought for the poor members of the church who had to make do with scraps (1 Corinthians 11) and exercised spiritual gifts to show off, rather than to serve others (1 Corinthians 12 – 14). As far as they were concerned, life in the Spirit was all about 'me': *my* freedom, *my* rights, *my* gifts.

Paul responds by reminding them throughout the letter that true spirituality is corporate: it is about 'us', the church. Christians belong together in a local church as the body of Christ, so the behaviour of each individual has an inevitable impact upon the others, for both good and ill. The Corinthians, therefore, should have realized that their accommodation of serious sin in their midst was bound to have a significant effect, not just on the individual concerned, but on the whole church. Hence Paul writes, 'Don't you know that a little yeast works through the whole batch of dough?' (5:6). Discipline was important, not just for the good of the individual, but also to prevent the spread of sin in the whole community.

The yeast of sin

In 1972, Cadbury's was forced to destroy 25 million chocolate Easter eggs because the yeast in the cream filling expanded after the eggs had left the factory and cracked the shells. That tragedy (as some might see it!) is a contemporary example of Paul's point in verse 6. Just as yeast spreads and grows, so sin expands in a church. If nothing is done when a church member is notoriously dishonest in his business dealings, continues to spread untruthful gossip about others or lives a sexually immoral lifestyle, the impression is given that it does not matter, and soon others are bound to follow, so that the yeast of sin begins to pervade the whole church.

Yeast was an obvious image for Paul to use because of its association with the Passover ritual (Exodus 12:17–20). At Passover time all the yeast had to be removed from each house before a lamb could be sacrificed as a reminder of God's rescue of the Israelites from the Egyptians at the time of Moses. That great rescue was a model of the perfect redemption achieved when Christ died in the place of others on the cross (just as the lamb had been killed instead of the Israelites' first-born sons). In the Passover ritual, the removal of the yeast precedes the sacrifice of the lamb. Paul uses the sequence of this familiar annual festival to stress the inappropriateness of allowing sin to take root in a church. Since Christ, the fulfilment of the Passover lambs, has already been sacrificed on the cross, it is high time Christians do all they can to remove the yeast of sin from his church. Paul commands the Corinthians, 'Get rid of the old yeast that you may be a new batch without yeast – as you really are. For Christ, our Passover lamb, has been sacrificed' (1 Corinthians 5:7). The implication should be clear for us. Far from turning a blind eye to public and persistent sin in our churches and denominations, we should take it seriously and, where necessary, exercise discipline to ensure it does not spread.

We are not to judge the world

Having made this point, the apostle proceeds to correct a misunderstanding that had arisen from what he had written in a previous letter. He had told the Christians 'not to associate with sexually immoral people' (5:9), meaning, 'anyone who calls himself a brother but is sexually immoral', or indeed, 'greedy, an idolater or a slanderer, a drunkard or a swindler' (5:11). They, however, understood Paul to be referring to unbelievers, so he puts them right: 'What business is it of mine to judge those outside the church? Are you not to judge those inside? God will judge those outside. "Expel the wicked man from among you"' (5:12–13).

All too often we Christians do the exact opposite of what Paul commands. We are quick to condemn the world, as I was when I joined a new football team a few years ago. I had not had close contact with non-Christians for a while, as I had been studying at Bible college, and was so shocked by my team-mates' language, drunkenness and attitude to women that I felt judgmental towards them and considered leaving. My instinct was to tell them off for their outrageous behaviour, but then I realized that, above all, the message I should seek to share with them should be a positive one about God's gracious love for them in Christ, and not just negative criticisms of their sins. It was certainly not my business to judge them; I should leave that to God.

While often being quick to condemn the world, and even withdrawing from it, despite Paul's clear teaching at the end of verse 10 that we should not do that, we are at the same time slow to take action against sin in the church. We may think we are being kind and compassionate, but in fact our compromise helps neither the individual nor the church. Sometimes, sadly, love demands decisive action against unrepentant serious sin. A sinful lifestyle is incompatible with the health of the church.

2. A sinful lifestyle is incompatible with the realities of the future (6:1–11)

Brothers at law

At the beginning of 1 Corinthians 6, Paul turns to another shocking example of the lack of distinctiveness in the Corinthian church. Christians were taking disputes between one another to unbelievers for judgment, rather than settling them among themselves (6:1). We are not told the details, but it seems from the words Paul uses in verses 7 and 8 that a church member had been 'cheated' and 'wronged' by another, and that the case had ended up in court. Paul is horrified and exclaims, 'One brother goes to law against another – and this in front of unbelievers!' (6:6).

The apostle underlines the inappropriateness of their behaviour by pointing them to what will happen in the future. This was an important emphasis because the Corinthians were focused entirely on the present. We saw in 1 Corinthians 4 that they thought they had arrived spiritually and had nothing more to look forward to – an attitude which prompted an ironic response from Paul: 'Already you have all you want! . . . You have become kings – and that without us!' (4:8). Later, in 1 Corinthians 15, we learn that some were even saying, 'There is no resurrection of the dead', believing that they had already been raised spiritually, and pointing, perhaps, to their ability to speak in 'the tongues of angels' (13:1) as evidence of their perfected state. No doubt this focus entirely on the present, excluding as it did any thought of a future day of judgment, contributed to the Corinthians' lax attitude to sin. But Paul counters this by pointing them to the realities of the future.

Christians will judge the world

Three times in 6:1–11 Paul asks the Corinthians, 'Do you not know?' (as he also does in 5:6 and 6:15). The Corinthians prided themselves on their great knowledge of spiritual matters, and Paul responds with more than a hint of sarcasm by asking them how, given that they are so knowledgeable, they could have forgotten such basic truths, including the fact that 'the saints will judge the world' (6:2).

Paul had taught them, when he was with them, that they were a community with a great future, called to belong to

God in the present age and to be with him in the age to come. As those who were united to Jesus Christ, their destiny was bound up with his: one day he would return to judge the world and, in him, they too would be involved in that judgment. Given that their destiny was to judge the world, they should surely recognize how inappropriate it was to hand over a dispute between two of their members to a court of this world. If they were to take part in a judgment of such huge significance, surely they should recognize that they were qualified to judge 'trivial matters', such as their own internal disputes (6:2b).

Paul's exasperation might be compared to that of the wife of a newly appointed High Court judge who ignores a row between his two daughters. As the screaming, scratching and hair-pulling continues, he refuses to get involved and expects his wife to deal with the problem until she shouts at him: 'You're about to be a High Court judge, making decisions on matters of national importance, so surely you should be able to sort out a petty dispute between our two children. Put your paper down, get out of your chair and do something!' In a similar way, Paul tries to shame the Corinthians into taking appropriate action: 'Do you not know that the saints will judge the world? And if you are to judge the world, are you not competent to judge trivial cases? Do you not know that we will judge angels? How much more the things of this life! Therefore, if you have disputes about such matters, appoint as judges even men of little account in the church! I say this to shame you.' (6:2–5).

Western society is increasingly litigious. There is a movement away from sorting out problems within the context of face-to-face relationships, instead delegating any matter or dispute to professional arbitrators or law courts. Lawyers advertise their expertise to those who have suffered any kind of injury, offering a 'no-win, no-fee' service. One church member recently sued her own church after slipping at a meeting in her pastor's home and spraining her ankle. She told him, 'It's nothing personal, but I'm told I could get some money.' Whatever we think of such behaviour in the world, it surely cannot be right within the church. We are family! We can sense Paul's exasperation: 'One **brother** goes to court against another – and this in front of unbelievers!' (6:6)

The church consists of sinful people, so it is inevitable that we will sometimes wrong one another. Often it will be best to turn the other cheek and make nothing of an offence against us. Sometimes, however, the wrong is too serious to ignore, and it will be right to take the first step outlined by Jesus in Matthew 18, and speak to our brother or sister about their sin, perhaps after discussing it beforehand with a wise and discreet friend. Whatever we do, we should make every effort to ensure that the problem is addressed within the church family and not outside it.

The wicked will be judged

Sin within the Corinthian church is not simply seen in the act of taking a Christian brother or sister to court, but also in the behaviour that led to that response, which Paul describes in verse 8: 'You yourselves cheat and do wrong, and you do this to your brothers.' Perhaps, for example, one church member sells an ox to another, knowing that it is in poor health and will soon die, and yet hides that information and still demands the full price. Such behaviour is not a one-off, but an example of a persistent pattern that prompts the solemn warning of verse 9: 'Do you not know that the wicked will not inherit the kingdom of God?' The implication is clear: Paul is warning the Corinthians that, if they carry on behaving in such a way, they too will be judged. He pleads with them, 'Do not be deceived: Neither the sexually immoral nor idolaters nor adulterers nor male prostitutes nor homosexual offenders nor thieves nor the greedy nor drunkards nor slanderers nor swindlers will inherit the kingdom of God' (6:9b–10). These sins are not mentioned because they are the worst possible evils Paul can think of, but rather because they are the sins which were in danger of taking root in Corinth (5:11; 6:8; 6:18).

The words translated 'male prostitutes' and 'homosexual offenders' most likely refer to the active and passive partners in homosexual intercourse. This reference to homosexual practice in a list of sinful behaviours is offensive to many in our culture. It is worth noting that Paul does not single out homosexuality as especially worthy of condemnation, but rather includes it in a list of sinful behaviour that also features heterosexual sin ('the sexually immoral' and 'adulterers'). The Bible's teaching that the only right context for sex is heterosexual marriage is challenging for all of us, whatever our sexuality. There is certainly no justification for any attitude or behaviour that implies that homosexual sin is worse than heterosexual sin. It is also worth stressing that the apostle is not condemning those who are tempted homosexually, any more than those who are tempted by heterosexual sex outside marriage. If this is an issue for you, do not let it become a lonely battle you face on your own, but share it with a trusted friend or pastor.[3]

Paul does not focus only on sexual sin, but also on other sins as well, such as swindling and slandering. His warning is not addressed to anyone who has ever sinned in these ways, but rather to those who persist in doing so, without any effort to repent. Those who claim to be believers and yet engage in a pattern of sinful actions without signs of regret or desire to stop provide no evidence that they are ready to meet their divine judge, so Paul warns them, 'The wicked will not inherit the kingdom of God' (6:10).

You were washed!

Paul's solemn words are not designed to rob the true believer of assurance. Christians who have repented of sin, trusted in Christ and seek to live a godly life can be sure that they are completely acceptable to God, despite the fact that they once lived like those described in verses 9 and 10. Paul reassures the genuine Christians in Corinth: 'That is what some of you were. But you were washed, you were sanctified, you were justified in the name of the Lord Jesus Christ and by the Spirit of our God' (6:11).

We too have done many terrible things, but now, if we trust in Christ, we are completely clean in God's sight, washed by the blood of the one who died for us. We have been 'sanctified', set apart from the wickedness of the world to live godly lives as God's people. We were under God's condemnation, but now we have been 'justified' and are completely in the right with him.

It is very important that we allow these glorious truths to sink in. The devil will do all he can to remind us of past sins, both those committed before and after we became Christians, and make us question whether God can really accept us after what we have done. He tells us, 'God is a holy God. You don't really think he'd welcome someone like you into his presence, do you? Of course everyone does wrong, but your wickedness is especially terrible.' It may be one particular deed that he keeps bringing back into our mind, a sexual sin perhaps, or some cruel act against another person, or he points to a long period of deliberate disobedience against God. At times our feelings of guilt can be overwhelming, but, no matter how dirty we feel, we should remember Paul's great words: 'You were washed!'

This glorious truth was underlined for a friend of mine when he was given a book called *The Private Memoirs and Confessions of a Justified Sinner*. When he looked inside, he found the pages were completely blank. God has wiped the slate clean for all who trust in Christ.

3. A sinful lifestyle is incompatible with the significance of the body (6:12–20)

A world obsessed with sex

The permissiveness of contemporary society is seen most obviously in its attitude towards sex. The old taboos have largely been swept away, with the result that the average age of the onset of sexual activity has been significantly reduced in recent decades, and the average number of sexual partners people have in a lifetime has greatly increased. Sex is everywhere: in magazines, on advertising billboards and television screens, and on the Internet. Pornography used to be confined to the top shelves in newsagents' shops, but is now just a few clicks away on our computer screens at home.

It is very hard indeed for Christians to resist sexual temptation in such a sex-soaked world, given that human desires are so strong in this area, and we are not nearly as distinct in our behaviour as we ought to be. A survey of 800 18- to 30-year-olds at Soul Survivor's Momentum Festival in 2009, of whom 99% were Christians, revealed that 31% had had full intercourse outside of marriage (ranging from 20% of 18- to 20-year-olds to 54% of 25- to 28-year-olds).[4] But, of course, it is not just young people who fall. Christians of all ages engage in sexually flirtatious behaviour, have affairs and view pornography.

'Everything is permissible for me'

We are not unique in living in a sexually permissive culture. Corinth, as we have seen, was known throughout the ancient world for its sexual licence, so much so that the very name of Corinth was used to speak of fornication ('Corinthianizing'). The pagan religions encouraged this behaviour. The goddess Aphrodite was worshipped as a prostitute, and her temple at the heart of the city was given over to debauchery. Sadly, it was not only the city that was permissive, but also the church. That is clear from the words that appear twice in verse 12, which are almost certainly a slogan used by a group within the church: 'Everything is permissible for me.' These words express the Corinthian pride in their freedom to do whatever they wanted. Such an extreme assertion of Christian liberty probably originated in truths Paul had taught them, which they then misunderstood and distorted. Perhaps they said, 'Now that we're in Christ, we're new creations who have been raised with him and been filled with his Spirit. As people of the Spirit, we've left the law behind – that belongs to our unredeemed life. We came to know Christ by grace, not by obeying the law; we've been set free from the law, so now we can do what we like. "Everything is permissible for us."'

That distortion of Paul's wonderful gospel of grace was combined with a sub-Christian view of the body, which owed more to Greek philosophy than to the teaching of the Bible. The Greeks believed that only a person's soul or spirit really mattered. Salvation, in their thinking, resulted in the release of the immaterial soul from the prison of the body to a disembodied state. The body, in contrast to the soul, was evil and would not last. It seems the Corinthians were influenced by such thinking and, as a result, had a low view of the body, which led some of them to conclude that no bodily action was spiritually significant, as it could not harm the pure spirit within. They therefore saw nothing wrong in sexual immorality, such as sleeping with prostitutes (6:15).

'Food for the stomach'

Another of the Corinthians' slogans appears in verse 13: 'Food for the stomach and the stomach for food.' They are making a direct parallel between eating and having sex. There is nothing immoral about having a meal and so, they believed, there is nothing immoral about having sex, even outside marriage, as it is just a bodily function.

This is still a common way of thinking today. In a recent programme about celibacy in the Roman Catholic Church, two priests admitted anonymously that they engaged in one-night stands, but insisted that these had no significance. One said, 'It's just a bodily release; it doesn't affect the real me'; another claimed that he was still celibate in his soul. Paul rejects any such suggestions that bodily actions are morally neutral and insists, 'The body is not meant for sexual immorality, but for the Lord, and the Lord for the body' (6:13b). In the verses that follow, he outlines a truly Christian understanding of the body which could not be higher. God, the Holy Trinity, has not only made our bodies, but has also redeemed them. Our bodies will be raised by God the Father, have been united with God the Son and are occupied by God the Holy Spirit. It is vital that we allow the Holy Spirit to convince us deeply of these truths if we are to resist the pressure we all feel to follow the world in our sexual behaviour.

a) The Christian's body will be raised by God the Father

There are no punctuation marks in Greek, so we cannot be sure when Paul is quoting someone else and when he is using his own words, but it seems likely that the quotation of the Corinthian view in verse 13 should not simply be, 'Food for the stomach and the stomach for food', but should also include the words, 'but God will destroy them both'. If so, the Corinthians were arguing that since God will destroy both food and the stomach, then, by implication, he will destroy sex and the body as well and, as a result, neither are significant to God. It is true that there will be no sex in the new creation as 'people will neither marry nor be given in marriage' (Matthew 22:30), but Paul is adamant that there will be bodies: 'By his power God raised the Lord from the dead, and he will raise us also' (1 Corinthians 6:14). Those words give us a preview of the truth he will expound in chapter 15. We cannot have a low view of the body once we remember that God not only raised Jesus physically, but he will raise us too: we will be physical beings in the new creation and not merely disembodied souls.

I have sometimes heard it said that 'God isn't very interested in what we do in our bedrooms'. But the Bible gives no justification for such a marginalization of the body, as if it had no spiritual significance. Christianity is the most earthy of religions. The God who made the whole material world is not just interested in our souls, but in our bodies as well. He made us sexual beings, and we are accountable to him for how we use our sexual organs.

b) The Christian's body has been united with God's Son

Paul continues to stress the moral significance of our bodies by reminding the Corinthians of a truth they should be familiar with: 'Do you not know that your bodies are members of Christ himself?' (6:15).

As Christians we are bound up with Christ: we are in him and he is in us. That is not just true of our spirits, but of our bodies too. They are joined to Christ already by the work of the Spirit, and one day they will be with him in the new creation in their risen forms. Given that our bodies are part of Christ's body, it should be unthinkable for us to put them to immoral purposes, and as Paul writes, 'Shall I then take the members of Christ and unite them with a prostitute? Never!' (6:15b).

A distinction is often drawn today between 'making love', which is sex in the context of a committed relationship, and 'having sex', which may be a one-night stand after meeting someone at a club or a chance encounter on a business trip. Whereas making love is regarded as being profoundly rela-tional, some argue that having sex is just a bodily transaction that means nothing. If you try telling that to your husband or wife, they will not be impressed. Paul too was appalled when some Corinthian Christians had sex with prostitutes and yet argued that it had no moral or spiritual significance. He responded, 'Do you not know that he who unites himself with a prostitute is one with her in body? For it is said, "The two will become one flesh"' (6:16).

Paul is quoting from Genesis 2:24, which outlines God's purpose for sex. In God's creation design, it is meant to form, express and strengthen the deep union of a man and a woman in lifelong marriage. There is, therefore, no such thing as 'casual sex', for that is a contradiction in terms. Paul is asking the Corinthians to consider what they are doing when they have sex outside marriage. Once we understand that our bodies are united with Christ, we should be horrified at the very thought of behaving immorally with them.

c) The Christian's body is occupied by God's Spirit

Paul once again has to remind the Corinthians of what they have already been taught: 'Do you not know that your body is a temple of the Holy Spirit, who is in you, whom you have received from God? You are not your own' (1 Corinthians

6:19). The Christian's body will not only be raised by God the Father, but is united by God the Son and occupied by God the Spirit. I must not think of the Spirit living just within a special part of me called the soul. I cannot separate myself from my body; I am a body-soul: a psychosomatic unity. When God lives in me, he lives in my body, and I must therefore live a holy life with my body.

How would our behaviour change if our husband, wife or some respected friend was with us every second of the day? Are there places we would not visit and things we would not do? Surely then the thought of the constant presence of the Holy Spirit with us should provide us with a much greater motivation to holy living? Paul urges us to apply this teaching, by both fleeing from sexual immorality (6:18) and honouring God with our bodies (6:20).

Flee from sexual immorality

The story is told of a bear that bumped into a hunter with a loaded gun. The bear put up his hands and said to the hunter, 'Come on, let's be reasonable – let's light a fire and chat a bit; you can tell me what you want and I'll tell you what I want.' 'All right,' said the hunter, 'I'm hunting bears because I want a great big fur coat.' 'That's fine,' said the bear, 'I'm looking for hunters because I want a great big square meal.' Fifteen minutes later the bear got up, patting his stomach contentedly. He had had his meal, and the hunter had got his fur coat on.

It's a silly story, but it does illustrate an important point. In some situations, wisdom demands that we flee, not negotiate; and that is certainly the case when we are tempted sexually. Too often we make a deal with sin, drawing some arbitrary line that we say we will not cross, but being prepared to compromise in what we think is a less significant way. Such behaviour is short-sighted because it fails to recognize the powerful pull sexual temptation exerts on us, so that, once we have started to succumb, it will be very hard to resist going the next step and then the next. It is also naive because it does not recognize the great damage that sexual sin inflicts.

Paul urges us to 'flee from sexual immorality' because 'all other sins a man commits are outside his body, but he who sins sexually sins against his own body' (6:18). It is not entirely clear what is meant by this statement, but it does surely assume that our sexual identity is not skin-deep, like a coat of varnish over the top of the body. It rather affects our innermost personalities, and especially so when we remember that, as physical beings, we are in a relationship with Christ. It is true that other sins, such as drunkenness, affect the body, but no sin has a greater impact on the ego, the inner person, than sexual sin.

Instinctively we know that sex is not simply a bodily trans-action, with no greater significance than eating or drinking; it is far more profound than that. In its God-ordained context of marriage, sex can bring great good, both through pro-creation and by expressing and deepening committed love. But when sex occurs in the wrong place, it can bring lasting damage physically (for example, through sexually transmitted infections), emotionally (perhaps in the sense of having been used and then rejected) and relationally (maybe because we hold back from commitment so as not to be hurt again after a previous sexual relationship that caused such pain).

What does the command to 'flee from sexual immorality' mean for us? Are we engaged in a sexual relationship that needs to stop? Have we allowed a friendship to develop into an inappropriate intimacy? Do we let our thought lives roam into sexual or romantic fantasies, fed by unhelpful books or films? Have we allowed pornography to get a hold on us, so that we keep being drawn back to sexually explicit Internet sites? Whatever our temptation, we must take decisive action to resist it.

We must not negotiate but rather flee. That will mean fleeing the situations which provide opportunities for temptation: leaving the party when everyone else is pairing off or the upstairs room when no-one else is around, or avoiding spending time on our own with the colleague to whom we are attracted. It will also mean fleeing the encouragements to sin: why risk watching those late-night programmes on our own, reading those borderline magazines or visiting that particular shop or part of town? Surely there is enough sinful desire coming up from within us without exposing ourselves to extra encouragement from outside? We will need to be especially careful with the Internet. Many have found it helpful to keep the computer in a public room in the house, or to ensure that an accountability partner sees all the sites they visit.[5] Let us determine that we will do whatever it takes, however costly, to run away from sin.

Honour God with our bodies

God will never let us keep spirituality in a box marked 'Sunday', 'Religion' or 'Soul'. He is interested in every day of the week, area of our life and part of our body. True spirituality is not just seen in how fervently we sing in church, but needs to be worked out in the details of our lives as we 'offer [our] bodies as a living sacrifice, holy and pleasing to God' (Romans 12:1), at home, school, college, the office or factory, and in our bedrooms as well. That will require that we do not just avoid sin, but strive to honour God in all that we do.

Bible study (1 Corinthians 5 – 6)

Read 1 Corinthians 5 – 6

1. In what different ways were the Corinthians exhibiting a lack of concern for holiness?
2. Are we any better today?

5:1–13

3. What is the situation Paul is responding to?
4. What principles do you learn about church discipline?

6:1–11

5. How should you respond when you are mistreated by another Christian?
6. How would you summarize:
   - the warnings of verses 9–10?
   - the encouragement of verse 11?

6:12–20

7. What false views does Paul counter?
8. What do you learn about a Christian view of the body?
9. What does it mean in practice to:
   - 'flee from sexual immorality' (verse 18)?
   - 'honour God with your bodies' (verse 20)?

Finally . . .

10. What have you learnt about true spirituality?
11. What alternative thinking does this challenge?

4. TRUE SPIRITUALITY
affirms both marriage and singleness, but not asceticism

(1 Corinthians 7)

Asceticism

Simeon Stylites is remembered by history as the fifth-century monk who spent thirty-nine years living at the top of a pillar, fifteen metres above the ground, in Syria. He was so determined to focus his thoughts and affections on God that he did all he could to cut himself off from the things of this world: seeking isolation from people, living on a subsistence diet and trying to avoid all thoughts of sex, to the extent that no woman, not even his mother, was allowed anywhere near him.

Simeon is an extreme example of ascetic spirituality. An 'ascetic', according to the Chambers Dictionary, is 'one who rigidly denies himself ordinary bodily gratifications for conscience's sake'. Asceticism is regarded as the ideal in some traditions of spirituality, in which celibates, who abstain from marriage, and hermits, who separate themselves from other people and from physical pleasure or comfort, are regarded as the greatest saints. However, the Bible does not support this mindset.

The goodness of God's creation

When the Lord Jesus commands us to deny ourselves and take up our crosses (Mark 8:34), he is not calling us to deprive ourselves of normal bodily pleasures, but rather to put his will above our own. He endorses fasting as a helpful discipline which can assist us in focusing on God in prayer (Matthew 6:16–18), but there is no suggestion that fasting should be a way of life rather than an occasional practice.

Paul spoke strongly against some in the first-century church who 'forbid people to marry and order them to abstain from certain foods', calling them 'hypocritical liars, whose consciences have been seared as with a hot iron' (1 Timothy 4:2–3). Such teaching is a denial of the goodness of God's creation. Once we remember that God is the great creator of the physical world, we are bound to resist any suggestion that truly spiritual people will seek to cut themselves off from the physical. God has provided the possibility of many wonderful physical pleasures in the world he has made, and it is a terrible ingratitude to deny ourselves the opportunity of enjoying them; that is the equivalent of a child perversely refusing to open a present. As Paul writes of the foods from which false teachers were encouraging Christians to abstain, 'God created [them] to be received with thanksgiving by those who believe and who know the truth.' He continues, 'For everything God created is good, and nothing is to be rejected if it is received with thanksgiving' (1 Timothy 4:3–4). That certainly includes God's gift of sex.

Created as sexual beings

We may be embarrassed about sex, but there is no prudery in the Bible. God created us as sexual beings; indeed, his first command to human beings in the Bible is, 'Be fruitful and increase in number' (Genesis 1:28), which is very hard to do without having sex, unless you are an amoeba. One whole book, the Song of Songs, speaks of the wonder of sexual love in marriage, and God's word has much to teach us about a right understanding of sex, not least in this chapter of 1 Corinthians, which is the longest section in the Bible devoted to issues related to sex and marriage. Its major themes of sex, marriage and singleness are of great interest to all of us, and it may well be that we approach this chapter looking for answers to particular questions which arise from our circumstances. Although we will certainly find guidance here for many contemporary issues, we should begin by remembering that Paul was writing initially into a specific situation. We can only apply his teaching appropriately to the twenty-first century once we have properly understood his message in the first century.

Is sex unspiritual?

In 1 Corinthians 7, Paul shifts from addressing issues that concerned him about the Corinthian church because of reports he had received about the situation there (1:11) to dealing with matters that arose from a letter he had received from the Corinthians. He begins, 'Now for the matters you wrote about' (7:1), and raises them in turn: sex and marriage (7:1); food sacrificed to idols (8:1); and spiritual gifts (12:1).

Paul begins his discussion of sex and marriage with the words, 'It is good for a man not to marry' (7:1). A more literal translation would be, 'It is good for a man not to touch a woman', or, as the alternative NIV translation puts it, 'It is good for a man not to have sexual relations with a woman.' Those words immediately confirm the suspicions of many that the Bible, and especially the supposedly repressed bachelor, Paul, is anti-sex, but that would be a serious misunderstanding of this chapter. It is best to understand these words not as Paul's own view, but as a quotation of a Corinthian view which the apostle then counters. As already observed, there are no quotation marks in the original Greek, so we can never be 100% sure when Paul is stating his own views and when he is quoting what others were saying. But it is clear that Paul does quote his opponents elsewhere in this letter, as we saw, for example, in 1 Corinthians 6, where we are surely right to understand the opening words of 6:12 as a quotation of a distorted view which Paul then counters: 'Everything is permissible for me.' The words 'It is good for a man not to marry' are best understood in the same way, as expressing the view not of Paul himself, but of others with whom he disagrees.

Paul is tackling some within the Corinthian church who taught that sex was inherently unspiritual. No doubt the origins of this view lay in the unbiblical understanding of the body which we encountered in 1 Corinthians 6, leading some to justify sleeping with prostitutes because they believed the body was spiritually insignificant. In 1 Corinthians 7 we find the same low view of the body being used to justify a completely contradictory position: asceticism. Some in Corinth, it seems, believed that because the body was inherently bad, the spiritual Christian should avoid bodily pleasures such as sex. As a result, it seems clear from what we read in chapter 7 that those who were married were feeling pressure to abstain from sex within marriage or even to abandon their marriages, and those who were single were being urged to avoid marriage. Such teaching may sound strange to us, but sadly there have been many Christians throughout the centuries who have given the impression that sex is, at best, a necessary evil, and that the most spiritual Christians will remain virgins. Paul strongly contradicts that view and insists that true spirituality affirms marriage. Having made that point, he does also affirm singleness very strongly, but, as we will see, this is certainly not because of any suggestion that sex is unspiritual or bad.

Sex is an obligation within marriage

Paul begins his response to the view of some that it was best for Christians to avoid sex by saying: 'But since there is so much immorality, each man should have his own wife, and each woman her own husband' (7:2). This appeal allows no exceptions: it applies to 'each' man and woman. It cannot, therefore, be addressed to single people, as that would directly contradict what Paul says later in the chapter when he urges many who are single to stay as they are, rather than get married (for example, 7:26). A more literal translation of verse 2 is, 'Each man should keep on having his own wife and each woman her own husband.'

The phrase 'having his wife' was never used to speak of getting, or taking, a wife, but was often used of sex. Paul is, therefore, addressing married couples who have ceased to have a sexual relationship because of a false view that sex is unspiritual, and tells them that they are asking for trouble. If, for example, a wife convinces herself that it is wrong to have sex, there is a danger that her husband will look for sex elsewhere. That might have been one of the reasons why some of the Corinthian men had begun to visit prostitutes (6:15–16). They were acting sinfully when they did so, but their super-spiritual wives were also partly to blame, so Paul says to married couples, 'Maintain your sexual relationship.'

The Bible is against marriage without sex

The point is spelled out even more clearly in 1 Corinthians 7:3–4: 'The husband should fulfil his marital duty to his wife, and likewise the wife to her husband. The wife's body does not belong to her alone but also to her husband. In the same way, the husband's body does not belong to him alone but also to his wife.' While the Bible is against sex without marriage, as we saw in 1 Corinthians 6, it is also against marriage without sex, assuming sex is physically possible.

The mutuality of Paul's words is striking: contrary to what is sometimes implied, we are not the first generation to recognize that women have sexual rights and longings. Paul instructs both husbands and wives to regard their bodies as belonging to the other and, by implication, to do all they can to satisfy their spouse sexually. That is a long way from our contemporary selfish attitude, in which sex is very often about 'me': maximizing *my* pleasure, *my* satisfaction and *my* fulfilment. By contrast, God wants us to understand sex not so much as something to be 'had', but as something that is 'given', as the husband and wife seek to satisfy each other.

There is nothing grudging about the Bible's attitude to sex. God does not say to married couples, 'Have sex if you must, but only to make babies and, even then, try not to enjoy yourselves.' In fact, he urges couples to have sex often, only refraining for a limited period by mutual consent, perhaps to enable a greater focus on prayer (7:5).

Many people express surprise that Christians decide to marry without any experience of sexual contact with each other, believing that couples should experiment beforehand, to see if they are sexually compatible. However, God's way is far better: within the security of the lifelong commitment of marriage, a couple can enjoy the adventure over many years, God willing, of making themselves compatible to the other's needs and desires, so that they grow in their sexual relationship as time goes by.

The Corinthians were saying no to sex even within marriage, but Paul counters and says that sex is an obligation within marriage. One friend of mine said that, before he was married, he found it hard to understand why any married couple would need to be encouraged to keep on having sex. Then, having been married for a while, he realized that Paul understood the dynamics of real marriage. There are many factors that threaten to kill, or at least stifle, romance and sex within marriage: tiredness, especially when there are small children in the house or work is demanding; unaddressed hurts or grudges that have been allowed to build up; illness or depression; preoccupations with worries and concerns; or over-busyness, so that a couple hardly have any uninterrupted time alone together. Sex is a very important part of a marriage, so couples should do all they can to keep sexual intimacy alive and mutually satisfying.

Every couple is different, and sexual desires change with age, so the application of Paul's teaching will vary. It might help for couples to talk together about what these verses mean for them, and even, if this is an area of real difficulty in a marriage, to seek the help of a trusted adviser. If you do not know how to raise the subject with your husband or wife, perhaps you could encourage them to read this chapter of the book and then start a conversation by saying, 'About that book . . . !'

Both marriage and singleness are gifts of God

Paul was unmarried and valued his single state so much that he could say, 'I wish that all men were as I am', but he knew that not everyone has the gift of singleness: 'Each man has his own gift from God; one has this gift, another has that' (7:7).

It is often assumed that Paul is referring to the particular ability that some have to be contentedly single. If so, very few single people beyond a certain age recognize themselves in this verse, as most have not chosen deliberately to remain unmarried and are conscious of the struggle involved through loneliness and a sense of unfulfilled longing for sexual intimacy. However, I am far from convinced that Paul is using the word 'gift' to speak of an ability. It is true that the same word does refer in 7:12 to abilities God has given to church members to enable them to edify others, but this word has a different meaning in other contexts. It is a general word that speaks of a gift of God's grace – even the gift of salvation, as in Romans 6:23: 'For the wages of sin is death, but the gift of God is eternal life in Christ Jesus our Lord' ('gift of God' translates the same word Paul uses in 1 Corinthians 7:7).

I believe the word 'gift' in verse 7 is most naturally understood not as the ability to be contentedly single or married, but rather as the state of singleness or marriage. Paul is grateful to God for his single state because of the great opportunities it gives him in Christian service, and wishes everyone could enjoy the same gift, but he does not go the next step and denigrate marriage by comparison, because he knows that marriage is also a good gift of God. That means that none of us is missing out. We all begin with the gift of singleness, then some replace it with the gift of marriage, before, in some cases, receiving the gift of singleness again after the death of a spouse. Both marriage and singleness have advantages and disadvantages, but both are gifts of God. Instead of focusing on what we do not like about our situation, we should, as far as possible, thank God for what is positive.

In our contemporary world, and often sadly our Christian world, which tends to devalue singleness, the immediate challenge is not to think, or imply to others, that singleness is second-best. In Corinth the immediate challenge was to those who were married and yet tried to mimic the single state by refraining from sex, because they regarded it as unspiritual. Paul rebukes them, reminding them that they do not have the gift of singleness. They are married, so they should thank God for the gift of marriage and maintain their sexual relationship within it.

Marriage may be preferable to singleness

If married people should accept the gift God has given them and not try to live as if they are single, should single people also simply accept their gift and never seek to change their status and become married? Paul addresses this question in verses 8 and 9. It seems likely that he is speaking in particular to those who have been married, but whose spouse has now died, as opposed to the 'virgins' who have never been married, whom he addresses in verse 25. However, the principles apply to any unmarried person.

Paul begins by commending singleness again: 'It is good for them to stay unmarried.' However, he certainly does not think that all single people should therefore remain single: 'But if they cannot control themselves, they should marry, for it is better to marry than to burn with passion' (7:9). Some react negatively to these words, believing them to reflect a low view of marriage which sees it simply as a refuge that should be sought, if necessary, to avoid sin. However, we should remember that this is not all the Bible says about the reasons for marriage. Elsewhere, marriage is affirmed as the right context for the bearing and raising of children, the loving partnership of a man and woman in the service of God, and even, in the loftiest possible terms, as a picture of the relationship between Christ and his church.[1]

Here, in 1 Corinthians, the focus is on marriage as the right context for sexual intimacy. Paul says that if the desire for such intimacy becomes overwhelming so that it is significantly distracting someone from single-mindedness as a Christian and, therefore, from making the most of the advantages of singleness, it may be time to consider marriage. Even then, an awareness of strong sexual desires is not, of course, the only factor to consider in deciding whether or when to marry, for if it was, many would need to get married at puberty. There are other factors to be considered as well, such as, 'Am I ready financially and emotionally for this commitment?', 'Are we really suited to each other, not least spiritually?' and 'Is this the man or woman I want to be the father or mother of my children?'

Some will no doubt be thinking to themselves at this point, 'These questions are hardly relevant for me. I find it very hard to control my sexual desires, but marriage is not a realistic possibility for me, whether in the short term because no-one is interested, or in the longer term because of a physical or psychological condition, homosexual orientation or other particular circumstances.' If so, however hard you find your situation, you can be sure that God understands and that he is with you by his Spirit to help you persevere as you seek to follow him. Not every single person does have a choice about whether to marry or not, but those who do should understand that they are completely free, and that often marriage is preferable to singleness.

Marriage is for life

A wit once remarked that marriage is like a besieged city: half the people want to get out and the other half want to get in. It was certainly the case that some in Corinth wanted to abandon their marriages, perhaps not simply because they thought they would be happier if they did so, but because they thought it was necessary to be really spiritual. Paul puts them right by commanding them to stay in their marriages: 'To the married I give this command (not I, but the Lord): A wife must not separate from her husband. But if she does, she must remain unmarried or else be reconciled to her husband. And a husband must not divorce his wife' (7:10–11). The apostle is summarizing the teaching of the Lord Jesus, as found, for example, in Mark 10:11–12: 'Anyone who divorces his wife and marries another woman commits adultery against her. And if she divorces her husband and marries another man, she commits adultery.'

Jesus' uncompromising teaching was not based, as some argue, on the cultural understanding of a different age, which no longer applies to our twenty-first-century society. His strong standards in this area were shocking in his own day, in which one Jewish rabbinical school argued that a man could divorce his wife simply on the grounds that she talked too loudly or burnt the supper, and when in the Gentile world all that was needed for a divorce was an oral or written notice and a couple of witnesses. Jesus based his teaching about divorce not on the standards of his contemporary culture, but rather on the principles of God's creation. In Mark 10, he quotes the words of Genesis 2:24, outlining God's creation design for marriage: 'For this reason a man will leave his father and mother and be united to his wife, and the two will become one flesh', and concludes, 'Therefore what God has joined together, let man not separate' (Mark 10:7–9). The basic principle is clear: marriage is for life.

Separation and divorce

However, Paul lives in the real world and knows that there are circumstances in which marriages do collapse, so after stating his principle that wives should not separate from their husbands, he includes the words, 'but if she does . . . '. There may be circumstances in which, because of physical violence or extreme psychological abuse, a wife may have to leave the marital home for her, or her children's, protection. Sadly, physical abuse is an all-too-common, although usually a hidden, problem within marriages, and victims should not suffer in silence, but seek help. Sometimes separation or divorce may be the lesser of two evils, but even then, the wife who leaves the marital home 'must remain unmarried or else be reconciled to her husband' (7:11).

Christians differ as to how they understand the additional words that appear only in Matthew's reporting of Jesus' teaching about divorce: 'Anyone who divorces his wife, **except for marital unfaithfulness**, and marries another woman commits adultery' (Matthew 19:9). The word translated 'marital unfaithfulness' is not the usual word for adultery and there is debate as to what exactly it refers, and also whether in these circumstances, whatever they are, only divorce is permitted, or remarriage as well. This discussion about the possibility of an exception should not cause us to lose sight of what is undoubtedly the basic principle: Jesus is against both divorce and remarriage, and urges husbands and wives not to divorce.

I am well aware that here, and indeed throughout this chapter, I am treading on very sensitive ground. It may be that you have personal experience of divorce; if so, you know more than anyone the pain it brings. Divorce is not an unforgivable sin, whatever the circumstances that caused it, so do not allow yourself to be overwhelmed with guilt or shame, but rather delight in the gospel and the promise of complete forgiveness in Christ. If you have remarried, and even if that new marriage should not have been entered in to, you should regard it as a binding covenant and pray that God will strengthen it. If you are not remarried, then, as far as it depends on you and assuming that your spouse has also not remarried, the basic principle is that you should seek reconciliation. That may not be a realistic possibility, at least in the short term, but it should be maintained as the ultimate goal.

Lifelong marriages require lifelong work

This teaching contains a strong encouragement to those who are married to work hard to keep their relationship strong. Some marriages break down, not because of any particular crisis, but because the couple gradually drifts apart over months and years. In one survey, 86% of divorcees revealed that the chief problem had been lack of proper communication. If marriage is for life, then couples must invest time and energy into maintaining their relationship over many years. Although all is well now, that does not mean there will be no challenges in the future, for example, when circumstances change with the arrival of children or the pressures of midlife, so no couple can afford to be complacent. Lifelong marriages require lifelong work.

Mixed marriages

The Bible is clear that Christians should marry Christians (1 Corinthians 7:39), but what if the Christian is married to a non-Christian, for example, if the former has been converted after marriage? Should that not provide an exception to the principle that Christians should stay in their marriages? It seems probable that some in Corinth argued that Christians in that situation should leave the marriage, because they were defiled spiritually through their union with an unbeliever. As this circumstance had not arisen in the Lord Jesus' ministry on earth, Paul is not able to refer to any of his teaching; so instead he gives his own instructions, which are no less author-itative, because, as an apostle of Christ, he speaks in Christ's name and with his authority. His teaching is clear: 'To the rest I say this (I, not the Lord): If any brother has a wife who is not a believer and she is willing to live with him, he must not divorce her. And if a woman has a husband who is not a believer and he is willing to live with her, she must not divorce him' (7:12–13).

Paul undergirds his principle with an explanation, in verse 14: 'For the unbelieving husband has been sanctified through his wife, and the unbelieving wife has been sancti-fied through her believing husband.' He is reassuring believers who are married to non-Christians that they are not defiled spiritually as a result; in fact, the opposite is the case, for the unbeliever is 'sanctified' through them. Sanctification here cannot mean salvation, as it is clear from verse 16 that the unbeliever in a mixed marriage may well not be saved. It seems most likely that Paul is using the language of ritual defilement from the Old Testament. When, for example, objects were set apart for God's use in the temple, they were designated 'holy'. If a holy object then came into contact with something unclean, it was defiled as a result. However, says Paul, in a mixed marriage the movement works the other way. Instead of the holy or 'sanctified' believer becoming defiled through sexual intercourse with a non-Christian, the unbeliev-ing husband or wife is 'sanctified' through their Christian spouse. The Christian should therefore stay in the marriage and not seek to leave it.

If 'sanctification' in this context does not mean that the unbeliever is saved, what is the significance of the concept? The end of verse 14 indicates that an important question in Paul's mind is how the children in a mixed marriage should be regarded. Paul teaches that they should be viewed not like the children of an unbelieving couple, but as if they had been born to two Christians. The implication seems to be that such children, along with the children of Christian couples, should be raised not simply as potential converts, but rather as members of God's family.

If you are a Christian married to an unbeliever, you will know the sadness and frustration that this can cause. Parenting can be especially difficult, because the beliefs and values you want to teach your children will be different from your spouse's. You should be encouraged by Paul's statement that they are regarded as in some sense 'holy' (verse 14), or 'set apart' by God, and do all you can to bring them up as Christians. This is a lonely situation to be in, and can be especially difficult if your partner is hostile to your faith and tries to stop you sharing it with your children. But even then, you should remember that spiritual incompatibility is not a justification for you to leave the marriage. You should rather stay and pray for your partner's conversion (7:16). It is usually best to resist the desire to try to speak too much to them about your faith, as that might turn them further away. Peter encourages Christian women, married to un-believers, to focus on being godly, so that husbands might be 'won over without words by the behaviour of their wives, when they see the purity and reverence of [their] lives' (1 Peter 3:1–2).

While Paul teaches that a believer in a mixed marriage should stay within it, he recognizes, however, that the un-believer may decide to leave. If so, the Christian should not feel bound to fight against separation or divorce to the bitter end. 'God has called us to live in peace' (1 Corinthians 7:15), and sometimes, reluctantly, peace is best served by a sad, quiet acceptance of the determination of the departing husband or wife.

The insignificance of circumstances

Verses 17–24 are central to all that Paul is saying through-out 1 Corinthians 7. Some in Corinth thought they would be more spiritual if they changed their circumstances, for example, moving from a sexual to a sexless marriage or pulling out of marriage completely. Such thoughts revealed that they were attaching far too much significance to circumstances.

From a worldly perspective, the circumstances in which we find ourselves matter very much. We instinctively have a scale in our minds which tells us that it is better to be a doctor than a shop-worker, a millionaire than one who struggles to get by on a pension, the owner of a five-bedroomed house than a tenant in a bedsit, and married rather than single. As a result, life for many people is a never-ending quest to better themselves by changing their circumstances, but that is to give those circumstances far too much importance. It is spiritually irrelevant whether we are rich or poor, employed or unemployed, blue-collar or white-collar workers. The Christian's energy should not be poured into seeking to change our life situation but, above all, into living the Christian life within it. Three times in this paragraph, in verses 17, 20 and 24, Paul states his basic principle: 'Each one should remain in the situation which he was in when God called him' (7:20).

Paul illustrates this principle with two examples: circum-cision and slavery. In the ancient world, the two great social divisions were whether you were a Jew or Gentile and slave or free, but Paul teaches that it does not matter either way. Those who were Jewish, or 'circumcised', when God called them to belong to Christ should remain Jewish, and Gentiles should stay Gentile. Our racial background has no spiritual significance, but 'keeping God's commands is what counts' (7:19). Similarly, those who were slaves at conversion should be content to remain slaves, although Paul encourages them to gain their freedom if that is a possibility (7:21). Identity is not a product of our racial, social or economic status, but rather of our relationship with God through Christ. The world may define someone first and foremost as a slave, but that person should rather see themselves as 'the Lord's freed man', set apart from the slavery of sin and death. In the same way, a free man should not take pride in his social position, but rather remember that, above all, he is 'Christ's slave' (7:22).

Our identity in Christ

It is very important to remember that our fundamental identity as Christians flows from who we are in Christ, and not from anything else. We too readily define ourselves in other ways: for example, as married, divorced, single, widowed, homosexual, childless or a single parent. All of these circumstances are significant, but we must not let them determine our sense of who we are. There is a danger that those who are happy in their situation will make an idol out of it and forget that their relationship with Christ must come before any other. This truth should also be an encouragement for those who are not happy in their marriage or singleness, and it provides a powerful antidote to the 'if only' thinking of our culture: 'If only I had a better home, was better looking, had a different job, did not have that elderly relative to look after, was married (or not married) . . . then I would be happy.'

God calls on us to accept our circumstances. Such contentment is only possible if we find our identity in Christ. Married Christians should remember that human marriage does not last for ever, and that the most important relationship in their lives is with Christ. Single Christians should also focus on him, and the eternal relationship with him that they can already enjoy in this world by the Holy Spirit, and which will be fully consummated when Christ returns to take his bride, the church, to be with him in the new creation. Armed with that attitude, we will be able to cope, with God's help, even when our circumstances are very difficult.

The Christian and singleness

From verse 25 Paul speaks to 'virgins', those who have never married, telling them that he has 'no command from the Lord', but will rather give 'a judgment'. He writes something similar in 2 Corinthians 8:8–10, where he chooses not to issue a command as Christ's apostle, as we saw he did in 1 Corinthians 7:12, but rather to give 'advice' (the same word that is translated 'judgment' in 1 Corinthians 7:25). We are free to choose whether or not to marry, so Paul does not command us one way or the other, but rather offers pastoral wisdom. It may be that he is especially addressing men who were already betrothed to be married, or the fathers of women who had been betrothed. Should they proceed with the marriage? Paul's words, however, are relevant for all who are considering marriage. He offers three pieces of advice:

- Keep eternity in mind: marriage is temporary (7:26–31).
- Face up to reality: marriage is complicated (7:32–35).
- Make your own decision: marriage is good (7:36–41).

Keep eternity in mind: marriage is temporary
There is much debate about how to understand Paul's words in verse 26: 'Because of the present crisis, I think that it is

good for you to remain as you are.' Does 'the present crisis' refer to a particular situation in Corinth, such as that alluded to in 1 Corinthians 11:30 where we learn that many church members have fallen sick and some have died? It may be that the church was facing an especially testing time but, if so, that does not mean that Paul's words do not apply to us. All that he says in this paragraph is relevant, not just to times of particular difficulty, but to the whole of the period until Christ returns. Paul encourages us to view history from God's perspective, recognizing that 'the time is short' (7:29) and that 'this world in its present form is passing away' (7:31). The apostle draws out the implications of these truths: 'From now on those who have wives should live as if they had none; those who mourn, as if they did not; those who are happy, as if they are not; those who buy something, as if it were not theirs to keep; those who use the things of the world, as if not engrossed in them. For the world in its present form is passing away' (7:29–31).

Paul is using rhetorical language, which should not be understood literally. Elsewhere he commands Christian husbands to love their wives 'as Christ loved the church and gave himself up for her' (Ephesians 5:25). Such sacrificial love is not possible under a literal reading of the instruction that 'those who have wives should live as if they had none'. Paul is simply saying that we should not live as if this world is all there is. For those who have no hope to look forward to, it is a disaster if they lose their job, become poor or do not get married; but Christians, knowing that this present world is not their ultimate home, are able to be relaxed about such things and not live as if these are the 'be all and end all' of life.

Many single Christians grow up with a calendar in their minds:

- Early to mid-twenties: meet the man or woman of my dreams.
- Late twenties: marry.
- Thirties: have children.

It is tempting to panic when our lives do not keep up with the timetable we have imagined, but we are not to live by our subconscious calendar, but rather by God's. Martin Luther used to say that he lived with two dates in mind: 'Today' and 'That day', the day when Christ will return to judge the world and introduce his perfect new creation. If we were to do the same, it would radically change our perspective on both marriage and singleness. Human marriage exists only in this present world, but our relationship with Christ will last for ever.

Face up to reality: marriage is complicated

Paul has a very high view of marriage as a wonderful gift of God, and yet he is also realistic about it, acknowledging that 'those who marry will face many troubles in this life' (1 Corinthians 7:28). Such honest talk is not often heard in Christian circles, which results in some single people believing the romantic myth that a couple meet, fall in love and then 'live happily ever after' (not 'even after' as in the misprint that appeared in one romantic novel!). Unmarried Christians can convince themselves, 'If only I was married, all my problems would disappear: I would no longer be lonely, have any insecurities or be tempted sexually.' Of course marriage does bring many blessings, but Paul wants us to know that, as well as solving some problems, it also creates others. He writes, 'I would like you to be free from concern. An unmarried man is concerned about the Lord's affairs – how he can please the Lord. But a married man is concerned about the affairs of this world – how he can please his wife – so his interests are divided. An unmarried woman or virgin is concerned about the Lord's affairs: her aim is to be devoted to the Lord in both body and spirit. But a married woman is concerned about the affairs of this world – how she can please her husband' (7:32–34).

Paul is not contrasting good and bad concerns, as if single people are more spiritual because they can devote themselves to the Lord's affairs. For those who are married, loving their spouse and their children is a demanding spiritual duty which has been commanded by God, and it should rightly take time and effort. As a result, their lives are more complicated than the lives of most single people. Quite rightly, their 'interests are divided' (7:34). We single people also have responsibilities to family members and friends but, as a general rule, we are pulled in fewer directions than those who are married and are therefore free to give more time to 'the Lord's affairs' (7:32), which might be sharing our faith with friends, discipling individuals, leading a Bible-study group or helping with children's work at church.

Paul is not against marriage, but simply wants the unmarried to enter it, if they do so, with their eyes wide open. For as long as we are single, whether that is a deliberate choice or not, we should focus not so much on those aspects of singleness that we find difficult, but rather on its advantages.

Make your own decision: marriage is good

Paul has pointed out some advantages of singleness, but we should certainly not conclude that those who stay single are especially spiritual; that would be to fall for the kind of teaching that was countered so strongly at the start of 1 Corinthians 7. Singleness is good, but so too is marriage, so single people are free to choose between the two. That is the point the apostle makes in verse 36: 'If anyone thinks he is acting improperly towards the virgin he is engaged to, and if she is getting on in years and he feels he ought to marry, he should do as he wants.'

Whether Paul is writing to engaged men, or to fathers who were unsure whether or not to marry off their daughters, as in the alternative NIV translation, his principles apply to all considering the possibility of marriage. We cannot be sure what is the impropriety, or shameful circumstance, that makes the man think he ought to marry. The word Paul uses literally means being 'over the top', and could refer either to the woman or the man. If the reference is to the woman, it speaks of her 'getting on in years', as in the NIV translation, as a result of which it is unfair for the man to keep her waiting any longer. If so, this is a challenge to men who continue in a relationship for a long time, while holding back from the commitment of engagement or marriage. That is not fair on the girl, so the time must come, sooner rather than later, either to get married or break up. However, I think it is more likely that Paul has in mind a man who is 'over the top', because he is finding it hard to control himself sexually within the relationship, and yet is holding back from marriage, possibly because of the influence of the ascetics who thought sex was unspiritual. Paul urges him not to be swayed by external pressure, but rather to 'do as he wants' (7:36).

Christians should marry only Christians

There are advantages in singleness, but as has already been pointed out, both marriage and singleness are good gifts of God, and so single people are free to choose. However, their choice is not unlimited. Paul's instruction to widows in verse 39 applies to all Christians: we should only marry those who 'belong to the Lord'. It surely follows that it is unwise to enter into a romantic friendship with a non-Christian, which, as it deepens, will lead either to the temptation to disobey God in marrying them or to the agony of a break-up. In my experience of pastoral ministry, I have seen more people drift backwards, or completely fall away, as a result of going out with or marrying a non-Christian than for any other cause. They have usually convinced themselves in the early stages of the friendship that they will not get very involved with the other person, but have then found that, as the attachment has grown, their resolve to do the right thing has weakened, until they have felt powerless to resist the strength of their emotions. They may comfort themselves with the thought that they may be used as a means of converting the one they love, and in God's grace that sometimes happens, but, sadly, on most occasions the influence works the other way. It is important, therefore, that we take heed to Paul's instruction: 'He [she] must belong to the Lord' (7:39).

Both marriage and singleness are good

This quick survey of 1 Corinthians 7 has not allowed me to deal adequately with the many delicate pastoral situations that underlie these issues. I apologize if you feel as if I have not given sufficient attention to your particular circumstance, or have dealt with it insensitively. I obviously do not know your situation, but God does, and you can look to him for wisdom and strength, knowing that he loves you as your Heavenly Father, has forgiven all your sins in Christ and will strengthen you daily by his Holy Spirit. As we focus on him, he will help us to have the right perspective on our singleness or marriage and see that status not as a problem, but as his gift and the context in which we can serve him both in good times and in bad.

Bible study (1 Corinthians 7)

1. What wrong thinking is Paul responding to in
   1 Corinthians 7?

7:1–7

2. What is Paul teaching about sex in marriage?

7:8–9

3. How do these principles apply to those who are
   unmarried?

7:10–16

4. What does Paul say about:
   • separation and divorce (verses 10–11)?
   • Christians married to non-Christians (verses 12–16)?

7:17–24

5. What principles lie behind what Paul writes?
6. How do they apply to how you view singleness and
   marriage?

7:25–35

7. What are the advantages of singleness?
8. How should the fact that 'the world in its present form
   is passing away' (verse 31) change your attitude to both
   singleness and marriage?

7:36–40

9. What do these verses teach those considering marriage?

5. TRUE SPIRITUALITY promotes spiritual concern, not unfettered freedom

(1 Corinthians 8 – 10)

Multiple choice

Multiple choice is a feature of all our lives. An academic at the University of Minnesota has concluded on the basis of extensive research that we all face between 300 and 17,000 decisions every day.[1] Some will be insignificant, such as which of the forty types of cereal we will choose in the supermarket, while others will be more important: which job will we do? Who should we marry? Where will we live? It is hardly surprising, given the number and complexity of the decisions we face, that we all, whether Christian or non-Christian, feel the need for help in this area.

Human beings have looked in all sorts of strange, and sometimes dangerous, directions for guidance: from animal entrails to tea leaves, from horoscopes to Ouija boards. Christians know that we must look to God, but how does he guide? Many are confused in this area and, as a result, otherwise rational people behave in bizarre ways, like the man who felt convinced he was called to be a missionary, but did not know where until he saw a large advert for Brazil nuts. One wonders what he would have done if he had seen an advert for Mars bars instead!

God guides us through the Bible

The basic principle we must understand if we are to be led by the Spirit in our decisions is that the Holy Spirit guides us supremely through the Bible. The Holy Spirit is the divine author of Scripture (2 Timothy 3:16) and still speaks through it today (see, for example, Romans 15:4 and Hebrews 3:7–8), so the Bible is not just a record of what God has said in the past, but is his living, contemporary word for us now (Hebrews 4:12). God tells us in the Bible all that we need to know to be able to discern the difference between right and wrong so we can live a life that pleases him. As Paul writes, 'All Scripture is God-breathed and is useful for teaching, rebuking, correcting and training in righteousness, so that the man of God may be thoroughly equipped for every good work' (2 Timothy 3:16–17). The key to discerning God's will, therefore, is to understand what the Bible says and then put it into practice. Very often our problem is not guidance but obedience. Everything that happens in our lives, even when we sin, takes place within God's sovereign will (represented by the outer circle in the diagram below),[2] as he is in complete control of everything, but we are called to live within the inner circle of God's moral will as we obey what he teaches in the Bible.

Freedom

The Holy Spirit uses the Bible to reveal God's moral will to us, but that still leaves us with many options. For example, a man contemplating marriage knows from Scripture that he

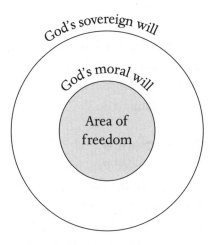

must marry someone of the opposite sex who is not already married and a believer, but that does not help him to decide between Susan and Samantha. The Bible takes us so far, but how does God guide us within the inner circle? Can we expect the Spirit to point us to his particular will for us – for example, to the exact person we should marry?

There are certainly examples in the Bible of God giving direct guidance in specific situations, such as when the Spirit told Philip to speak to the Ethiopian eunuch (Acts 8:27–30), or when Paul received a vision of a Macedonian man begging him to go and preach the gospel to his people (Acts 16:9), but those were unusual and unexpected occasions. It is clear from reading the New Testament that the early Christians assumed the normal pattern within the circle of God's moral will was that they had decisions to make rather than discoveries. They understood that God had given them freedom, and that their responsibility was to pray for the Spirit's help to make choices wisely rather than listen for his direct instructions. We read of frequent examples of them weighing up the alternatives and then coming to their own decisions, saying, for example, 'We thought it best' (1 Thessalonians 3:1); 'It would not be right for us' (Acts 6:2); and 'I think it is necessary' (Philippians 2:25). Theologian Jim Packer has concluded, 'The inward experience of being divinely guided is not ordinarily one of seeing signs or hearing voices, but rather one of being enabled to work out the best thing to do.'[3]

Questions of conscience

In 1 Corinthians 8 – 10 we find Paul instructing the Corinthians how to make decisions in particular matters that were within the area of freedom (the inner circle in the diagram). He does not tell them what to do, but he does teach them important principles that will help them make godly decisions. They are not to focus on themselves and their freedom, but rather to think of the spiritual impact of how they live. The principles he teaches still have a wide application to us today, as we try to work out the godly way to behave in matters where there is no direct command from God.

The challenge of making decisions in the area of freedom can be illustrated by looking at the different approaches of two imaginary young men: Simon and Tom. Like many others of their age, they lived for the weekend. Every Friday and Saturday night they would go out on the town, starting in a pub where they would smoke and drink with friends, before moving on to a club where they would dance until the small hours. Then, within a few weeks of each other, both were converted. Simon immediately turned his back on his old way of life, gave up smoking and alcohol, and now steers clear of pubs and clubs; he does not want anything to do with his former life that had led him so often into sin. Tom's behaviour also changed. He does not get drunk or pick up girls for one-night stands and he refuses drugs when he is offered them, but he still smokes, drinks alcohol and goes clubbing with his friends at weekends. 'I am free to do all those things,' he says. 'After all, there's plenty of alcohol and dancing in the Bible, and I don't know any biblical principle that condemns smoking.' When his friends remind him that 'his body is a temple of the Holy Spirit', he replies, 'I suppose that means you never eat a cream cake', which usually keeps them quiet. 'How can I reach my friends for Christ if I'm never with them?' he asks. Simon is shocked by Tom's behaviour: 'Surely, by going to such places, he is condoning the sin that takes place there and runs the risk of being seduced back into it himself?' In his view, Tom is being worldly with his smoking, drinking and clubbing. Tom, on the other hand, feels sorry for Simon and tries to persuade him that he is wrong: 'If only he knew his Bible better, Simon would realize that he is not bound by legalism any more, because Christ has set him free.' Sometimes, before going out on a Friday evening, Tom even rings his old friend and encourages him to come along too.

Who is right, Simon or Tom? There is nothing new in differences of opinion like theirs. Many churches have tensions within them between what we might call a 'libertarian group', which asserts its freedom, and a 'conscience group', which is much more cautious, each thinking they are more spiritual than the other. Such a division emerged in Corinth over the issue of food sacrificed to idols, which is the next subject Paul addresses from the letter he had received from the church in Corinth.

The libertarians insisted they were free to eat meat sacrificed to idols, while the conscience group was horrified by the very thought of doing such a thing. It seems that the libertarians were the dominant group in Corinth and were selfishly determined to express their freedom, regardless of the impact on others. Paul did not fit neatly into either camp, but he did agree with much of what the libertarians were saying. The Christian life is not a matter of obeying lots of little rules and regulations, and we do have great freedom as Christians within the limits set by God's word. However, just because the Bible does not condemn an action does not necessarily mean we should engage in it. Often it is right to rein in our freedom for the sake of our own spiritual health or that of others. True spirituality promotes spiritual concern, not unfettered freedom.

Paul's teaching here can be applied beyond the particular matter of eating food sacrificed to idols to the issues facing Tom and Simon, and indeed to all the different decisions we face as we seek to live a godly life today. We are taught three important principles that apply to all Christian decision-making, especially in the matters which are not covered in a clear command from the Bible:

1. Love is more important than knowledge
   (1 Corinthians 8).
2. The gospel is more important than rights
   (1 Corinthians 9).
3. Spiritual health is more important than freedom
   (1 Corinthians 10).

1. Love is more important than knowledge (1 Corinthians 8)

Meat sacrificed to idols

Paganism pervaded every aspect of life in the ancient world. Temples to different gods were at the heart of the cultural and social life of each community, so it was very hard for Christians to avoid some contact with idolatry, especially with regard to food. Most of the meat that was consumed had been butchered by priests in the context of pagan rituals. Should Christians buy and eat such meat when it was sold in the marketplace?

That is the question Paul deals with at the end of 1 Corinthians 10. The particular issue addressed in chapter 8 seems to be the question of whether or not Christians should eat such meat in an idol temple (8:10). Pagan shrines were the restaurants and nightclubs of the first century and formed an integral part of the social life of the day. Those who were celebrating a birthday or wedding were likely to invite their friends to the local temple to share in a meal. This would have been a mainly social event, although there was a religious element too, as the meat that was eaten would have been sacrificed to an idol. Should Christians ever attend such meals?

Paul begins his response by saying, 'We know that we all possess knowledge' (8:1). It is likely he is quoting a slogan of the libertarian group at Corinth. They were proud of their theological understanding and were confident that, because idols had no substance and food was spiritually insignificant, it was fine for them to eat in an idol's temple. Paul agrees with their presuppositions, acknowledging that 'an idol is nothing at all in the world' and that 'there is no God but one' (8:4). Idols are just bits of wood and stone, which have no real existence, in contrast to the only true God, the Father, and his Son, the Lord Jesus Christ (8:6). Paul also agrees that 'food does not bring us near to God' (8:8). It makes no difference to our spiritual life whether we eat chocolate in Lent, fish on Fridays or consume meat that has been previously offered to an idol. However, even if we may be free to eat anything we like, that does not necessarily mean that we should. Paul may agree with the libertarians' theology, but he certainly disagrees with their selfish application of it.

'Knowledge puffs up'
Knowledge or theological learning is not the only factor to take into account when making a decision. As Paul stresses

right at the start of the chapter, 'Knowledge puffs up, but love builds up' (8:1). The word translated 'puffs up' appears six times in this letter, but only once in the rest of the New Testament.[4] It speaks of the spiritual pride which is one of the characteristics of the Corinthian church.

Those who have a good knowledge of the Bible's teaching are especially prone to spiritual pride. Perhaps we hear a passionate preacher who clearly loves Christ and exhorts his hearers to love him too, but, instead of heeding the message, we are quick to criticize, saying to a friend, 'I didn't like his handling of the passage at all. He failed to put the verses in context and completely missed the main point.' Or when we are with other Christians from different backgrounds praising God at a conference, we stay aloof in our hearts and think to ourselves, 'How can they sing that song? It's theologically vacuous. And I wish they wouldn't keep on talking about "worship" as if it was just singing rather than the whole of our lives offered to God.' We may have a point, but before we judge others, we should remember that God is more concerned with the love (or the lack of it) in our hearts than the knowledge in our heads.

'Love builds up'

The priority of love should apply not just to our attitudes, but to our actions as well. Our theological understanding may rightly tell us that we are free to take a particular course of action, but that does not necessarily mean we should follow it. Our freedom must be exercised lovingly and, if necessary, curbed. Paul urges the libertarians at Corinth to make sure that they do not express their freedom in such a way that it causes 'a stumbling-block to the weak' (8:9), for, he says, 'If anyone with a weak conscience sees you who have this knowledge eating in an idol's temple, won't he be emboldened to eat what has been sacrificed to idols? So this weak brother, for whom Christ died, is destroyed by your knowledge' (8:10–11).

Paul is concerned for a Christian whose conscience will not let him eat meat that has been sacrificed to an idol. If he sees another believer doing so, and is even encouraged to join in, he may end up succumbing and, as a consequence, do something that his conscience tells him not to do, which Paul therefore regards as a sin. In his letter to the Romans the apostle discusses a similar issue and writes, 'But the man who has doubts is condemned if he eats, because his eating is not from faith; and everything that does not come from faith is sin' (Romans 14:23). It is possible that this sin against his conscience may have even more serious consequences if the 'weak' Christian is sucked back into their old idolatrous ways as a result of eating in a pagan temple. Paul therefore makes his own resolution, which he expects all in Corinth to follow: 'Therefore, if what I eat causes my brother to fall into sin, I will never eat meat again, so that I will not cause him to fall' (8:13).

Sins against conscience

The implication of Paul's teaching is that sin is a broader concept than we often think. We sin not only when we disobey the clear instructions of God's word, but also when we do something which our conscience tells us not to do. Even when both the Bible and our conscience allow us to behave in a certain way, we still sin when we do it, if the result is that a Christian brother or sister sins against their conscience, having been emboldened to do so by our behaviour. Love demands that we rein in our freedom in such circumstances. That may mean, for example, not drinking alcohol in the presence of a teetotaller, not talking about a film we have seen in front of someone we know who disapproves of it, or not going into a shop on a Sunday when we are with a strict Sabbatarian.

However, we must not misunderstand this teaching as a justification for allowing a small group of brothers and sisters to block every proposed change in a church. Paul is not saying that we should never do anything that might hurt the feelings of others or offend their sensibilities. The issue is not whether our behaviour might cause upset, but whether it could lead other believers to sin against their conscience. Some church members may not agree, for example, with a decision to replace pews in a church building, but it is hard to imagine that they will be led into sin if it goes ahead. If the opposition is deeply felt and widespread, it may be wise to delay, or even cancel, the proposed removal, but it would not be right to appeal for such a course of action on the basis of 1 Corinthians 8.

What does this chapter of 1 Corinthians have to say to Tom and Simon? Even if Tom's conscience allows him to go to pubs and clubs, he should surely not encourage Simon to join him. And if Simon is visiting him one evening, love demands that Tom stays in with him to watch *The X Factor* on television, rather than engaging in his normal Saturday activities, so as to avoid any possibility of leading his brother into sin. He may know that there is nothing inherently sinful about going to a pub, but love is more important than knowledge. As one preacher put it, 'When God measures a person, he puts the tape round the heart, not the head.'

2. The gospel is more important than rights (1 Corinthians 9)

'I know my rights'

'I know my rights,' shouts the criminal as he is bundled into the police van. We all know our rights these days. This focus on rights came to prominence in the words of Thomas Jefferson in the American Declaration of Independence in 1776 with its reference to the 'inalienable rights to the preservation of life and liberty and the pursuit of happiness'. The United Nations Declaration of Human Rights is now increasingly adopted around the world and, in the decades since it was first issued in 1948, we have heard much about women's rights, gay rights and children's rights. There is much that is good about this emphasis on human rights, which owes a great deal to the Bible's teaching that every individual is created in God's image (Genesis 1:27), with equal dignity and worth. However, while we Christians will often want to plead vigorously for the rights of others, we should not always seek to uphold our own rights. Paul teaches clearly in 1 Corinthians 9 that the Christian way often involves giving up our rights for the sake of others.

In 1 Corinthians 8, Paul has taught the Corinthians that, although they might be free to take a particular action because neither the Bible nor their conscience forbids it, sometimes out of love for others they should forgo their right to do it. In chapter 9 he offers himself as an example for them to follow. He had the right to receive financial support for his ministry when he was in Corinth, but he gave up that right and did not ask for any money, out of a selfless love for others.

Paul begins the chapter by asking, 'Am I not free? Am I not an apostle?' (9:1). The Corinthians doubted both those facts about him. He certainly was not what they expected of an apostle who had been especially commissioned by Christ. We have noticed already that they were familiar with philosophers, who would travel from town to town, offering their particular brand of wisdom for life, some even becoming celebrities because of the attractiveness of their message and the brilliance of their communication skills. Just as film stars can be ranked according to how large a fee they can demand, the importance of these speakers was judged by how much they were able to charge. And yet, when Paul was staying with the Corinthians, he asked for no pay, but rather earned his own living by working as a tent maker. It was so undignified, they thought, for someone who claimed to be an apostle to work with his hands! Surely if he really was an apostle, he would know what he was worth and expect proper payment, just as other Christian leaders had done when they passed through Corinth?

Paul defends himself by stressing that he knows his right as an apostle to be materially supported in his ministry (9:3–6), as was clear both from the Old Testament (9:9–12) and from Jesus himself, who taught that 'those who preach the gospel should receive their living from the gospel' (9:14). However, he tells the Corinthians, 'we did not use this right' (9:12) and, in case they think he is dropping them a hint that he wants to receive payment in the future, he stresses, 'I am not writing this in the hope that you will do such things for me' (9:15). He is determined to continue with his policy of not claiming his right to financial support, so as not to 'hinder the gospel of Christ' (9:12).

'I make myself a slave to everyone'

No doubt there were many in the first century who preached a religious message with the pretence of spirituality, but were in fact only interested in lining their own pockets. Paul was worried that people might think that he too was motivated by a desire to make money if he asserted his right for support, and that they would consequently not take his message seriously, so he did not ask for the wages that were his due. He might be missing out on a more comfortable lifestyle as a result, but that did not bother him, for the only 'reward' he was interested in was being able to preach the gospel without doing anything that might make it harder for others to accept it. That attitude did not just apply to this decision, but governed his whole lifestyle. He wrote, 'Though I am free and belong to no man, I make myself a slave to everyone, to win as many as possible' (9:19). He is following the example of his master who, although he was 'in very nature God, did not consider equality with God something to be grasped, but made himself nothing, taking the very nature of a servant' (Philippians 2:6–7).

'All things to all men'

It is likely that Paul's opponents accused him of inconsistency, as they wondered how he dared pronounce on the matter of food sacrificed to idols and tell others what to do when he himself did not seem to have made up his mind on such matters. After all, on some occasions he played the good Jew and strictly observed kosher regulations, but at other times he ignored them. Was he a weak character who succumbed to peer pressure and simply fitted in with whoever was with him at the time? Or was he theologically unclear, having not fully understood that he was free from the cultural demands of the Jewish law?

In response, Paul insists that he is not being inconsistent. In fact, he always stuck rigidly to his principle that the gospel is more important than rights. As a result of that principle, he was prepared to give up his rights and adapt to the sensibilities of others, so as to avoid putting up unnecessary barriers that would prevent people from hearing the gospel. Therefore he says, 'To the Jews I became like a Jew, to win the Jews' and 'To those not having the law [the Gentiles] I became like one not having the law . . . so as to win those not having the law . . . I have become all things to all men so that by all possible means

I might save some' (1 Corinthians 9:20–23). Paul was a chameleon for Christ. He would never compromise on issues of morality or truth, and he never used underhand, deceitful methods of evangelism, but, if there were any cultural factors that got in the way, he was determined to be the one to adapt, rather than expecting non-Christians to do so. So, if he went to a Jewish home, he ate kosher food, although he knew that he was free not to; and if he went to a Gentile home, he ate whatever was put in front of him.

The Corinthians were individualistic. Their concern focused on themselves: '*my* freedom', '*my* rights'. That is one of the many ways in which the Corinthian mindset is very contemporary. We belong to a generation of individuals who are conscious of our rights and are quick to assert them, but Paul is clear that, as Christians, we are to be concerned not for ourselves above all, but for others. Even when God's word and our conscience tell us we are free to do something, we should still refrain from doing it, if it might have a negative effect on other Christians (1 Corinthians 8), or on non-Christians (1 Corinthians 9). The gospel is more important than rights, so we should not ask simply, 'What am I free to do?', but also, 'What will make it easiest for others to hear the gospel?' In going to pubs and clubs, therefore, Tom has a right concern for his friends. How can he reach them with the gospel if he is never with them?

Paul's example does not mean that all Christian workers should give up their right to payment for their ministry. The Bible stresses that they should be adequately paid, and Paul himself was often happy to receive such support (for example, in Philippians 4:14–18). He only gave up his right in situations where he feared that his receiving money might provide an excuse for non-believers to discredit him and not take his message seriously. Such occasions are likely to be rare, although excessive payment of evangelists and pastors can cause a stumbling block to non-believers. The preacher who drives a Rolls Royce, wears expensive jewellery and lives in a mansion is bound to be suspected of preaching to make money rather than to commend Christ. But while excessive payment is sometimes a problem, inadequate provision for pastors is perhaps more common. Denominational officials, elders and church councils should take care to provide reasonable support for their ministers, and avoid paying either too much or too little. Gospel workers have the responsibility of doing all they reasonably can to ensure that nothing about how they receive or spend money could create an obstacle.

Living for others

Paul's example of becoming all things to all men contains many challenging applications for us. It should be obvious that, although we are free to drink alcohol, and women are free to wear off-the-shoulder dresses, we should forgo those rights when we are trying to build a friendship with a Muslim, just as we would not serve bacon sandwiches if we invited a Jewish friend for a meal. But the challenge of 1 Corinthians 9 extends far beyond what we eat or wear, and forces us to ask whether we live above all for ourselves or, under Christ, for others. 'Do I share Christ's concern for the lost? If so, am I prepared to make costly decisions for the sake of seeking to win them?'

Contemporary spirituality tends to be self-indulgent, chasing after experiences that make one feel good about oneself, and has little place for the cross except as an attractive ornament. True spirituality by contrast, as modelled supremely by the Lord Jesus, makes sacrifices for the spiritual benefit of others. That is what motivates missionaries to give up their right to a comfortable life in the country of their birth, surrounded by family and friends, to cross cultures so they can reach the unreached with the gospel, and it is what spurs wealthy Christians not to use their freedom to spend money ensuring their lives are as luxurious as possible, but rather to have only a modest lifestyle so they can give as much as possible to support gospel work. We need to ask, 'In what ways does our love for the lost lead us to curb our freedom and forsake our rights?'

Leaving the Christian ghetto

As society becomes increasingly secular, it is tempting for us believers to retreat into a Christian ghetto, or sub-culture, rather like a rabbit warren beneath where most people live. We emerge into the real world when we have to, to go to work or do the shopping, but we ensure that almost all our social interaction takes place where we feel safe, with other believers. From time to time our church organizes an evangelistic event and we reluctantly go out to try to persuade some non-Christians to attend. Unsurprisingly, most say no: they hardly know us, and, when they do peer down into the rabbit warren below, they are put off by the strange jargon we use, the clothes we wear and the songs we sing. Our world is alien, and they are sure they would feel out of place if they entered it. So we retreat back to our friends to report that evangelism is very hard these days, and then return with relief to our comfortable life with our fellow Christians.

That is a caricature, of course, but there is enough truth in it to make us uncomfortable. We are free to spend all our time with Christians, but we cannot expect to see colleagues and neighbours show any interest in Christ if we do not to some extent share our lives with them and show an interest in what interests them. For some of us that might mean attending fewer Christian meetings so that we can get involved in a sports club, play in an orchestra or serve as a school governor. When we do socialize with non-Christians, we should do all we can to avoid creating unnecessary barriers. Do we really need to say a long, loud grace in the restaurant and then launch into a lecture about the potential dangers of Harry Potter books or the musical merits of our favourite Christian band?

There is a challenge for churches as well. Jesus told his disciples to 'go and make disciples of all nations' (Matthew 28:19), but we have turned the 'go' into 'come'. Instead of making an effort to reach people where they are, all too often we do little more than put a notice on the church door with the times of our meetings and wait for them to arrive. If they do turn up, we expect them to take us as they find us, rather than adapting as far as possible to make it easy for them to hear the gospel. But we need to recognize that, if we are to reach people, we must go to them rather than expecting them to come to us. I can think of many impressive examples of churches doing just that, for example, by running after-school clubs for children, encouraging members to join prison-visiting teams, organizing regular events in residential care homes, teaching English to immigrants or offering parenting classes. The needs and opportunities will vary depending on our context, but perhaps we could start by asking which different groups of people live in the neighbourhood. How could we build bridges with them? What could we do to serve them? What would be the most appropriate way to share the gospel with them? We are not free to adapt the gospel message, which has been entrusted to us by God, or to lower our standards of integrity, but that still leaves a large area of freedom in which we should be driven not by our own desires, but by a concern for others. The gospel is more important than rights.

3. Spiritual health is more important than freedom (1 Corinthians 10)

Legalism or licence?

About sixty years ago, a leader of the Christian Union at Oxford University went into one of the colleges to ask a student if he would be willing to serve as president for the next year. He saw him playing croquet and, without saying anything, immediately turned round and left. The problem was that it was a Sunday and, in his view, someone who played croquet on the Sabbath was clearly not a suitable candidate for Christian leadership.

Christian culture has changed dramatically since those days. We have reacted against what we regard as the legalism of a previous generation, but now there is a danger that we have moved from excessive legalism to excessive licence. Whereas many of our Christian forbears regarded all movies with suspicion and never went to the cinema, we, by contrast, are prepared to watch almost anything on television or on the big screen. If it was true that they placed too wide a berth between themselves and the world, are we not often guilty of steering too close to the wind? That was certainly the danger for some in Corinth.

Go for gold!

Having presented himself as an example of the Christian way of living in giving up rights for the sake of others, Paul is about to return to the issue the Corinthians had raised about eating meat sacrificed to idols (1 Corinthians 10). In chapter 8 he partially agreed with those who argued that there was no theological principle which prevented them from eating food in an idol temple, but in chapter 10 he warns them strongly against the practice, pleading with them to flee from idolatry. He was concerned that, by using their freedom as they did, they were putting themselves in a perilous position and in danger of drifting back into their old idolatrous past. He urges them instead to copy the self-discipline of athletes in their efforts to avoid sin (9:24–27).

My ambition as a child was to be a great sportsman. I used to dream of winning Wimbledon, hitting a century at Lords and scoring a grand-slam winning try for Wales, all in the same year. My favourite book at the time was called *The Way to the Top*, in which some of the greatest sports stars of the day described how they had achieved their goals. What they wrote was both inspiring and very daunting. It was soon clear to me that, if I was to make it as a sportsman (sadly never more than a totally unrealistic childhood dream), I would have to work very hard indeed. All the stars described long hours of training and practice over many years, before they ever began to realize their potential.

Paul refers to this disciplined effort of athletes in 9:25 and uses it as a model for our lives as Christians. Athletes commit themselves to months of arduous preparation, all for the sake of 'a crown that will not last' (9:25), the victor's laurel wreath or gold medal. By contrast, the crown we will receive as Christians 'will last for ever' (9:25), so Paul appeals to us to 'run in such a way as to get the prize' (9:24). We are not to be like those who enter the London or New York Marathon simply for the experience, and only do enough training to ensure they will be able to finish without having a heart attack; rather we should be living the Christian life wholeheartedly, like the élite athletes who invest the utmost effort to give themselves the best possible chance of winning.

Paul offers himself to the Corinthians as a model of such self-discipline: 'Therefore I do not run like a man running aimlessly; I do not fight like a man beating the air' (9:26). He is not like a man on a jogging machine in the gym, going nowhere, or a shadow boxer pretending to fight. He is not playing at being a Christian, but has his eyes fixed on the prize of being with Christ in eternity once he has finished his race on earth, and he is determined that absolutely nothing will deflect him until he gets to the finishing line. He uses vivid language to describe his self-discipline: 'I beat my body and make it my slave so that after I have preached to others, I myself will not be disqualified for the prize' (9:27).

Paul is certainly not suggesting that we must earn salvation by our own efforts. It is by God's grace that we begin the Christian life, and it will only be through his grace that we will stay Christian. However, the wonderful truth that God will ensure that his people keep trusting in Christ until the end must never be used as an excuse for complacency. If I make no effort to live distinctively, there is no evidence that my faith is genuine and that I really do belong to Christ. So I must never coast in the Christian life, but rather, like an athlete in training, exercise rigorous self-discipline as I fight against sin and strive to live wholeheartedly for Christ.

These verses introduce another principle which guided Paul's decisions: spiritual health is more important than freedom. This is an important balance to the principle we have seen in 9:1–23 that the gospel is more important than rights. The libertarians no doubt emphasized the importance of adapting to non-Christians, and used that principle to support their practice of eating in idol temples; they might even have said, 'We need to be in the world to win the world.' Paul certainly agreed with them at that point, but he also warns them to be careful, because they were behaving in ways that put their spiritual health, and even their very salvation, at risk.

While some Christians should get into the non-Christian world more often than they do, others need to be warned to retreat from it, because of the spiritual danger they are in. The pressure points will vary for all of us. We need to be aware of our weaknesses and be on our guard in those areas. I may be free to read that book, watch that film, go to that party, accept that job and spend time with that friend, but, if I know that doing so will make it very hard for me to resist sin, I will need to restrict my freedom. It will require self-discipline, which may be very costly, but it will be worth it. If the athlete is prepared to go to great efforts for a prize that does not last, surely Christians will be prepared to make sacrifices for the sake of our eternal inheritance with Christ?

A warning from history

Paul underlines his appeal to strive to be godly by reminding the Corinthians of Old Testament history. Many of them were complacent, confident that all was well between them and God. It seems from what Paul says at the beginning of I Corinthians 10 that much of their assurance was based on their participation in the sacraments. They thought that, because they had been baptized and received the Lord's Supper, their salvation was assured, no matter how they behaved. However, Paul knew they were in grave spiritual peril because of their participation in meals in pagan temples, which threatened to suck them back into idolatry and away from Christ, so he tries to shake their false assurance. He does so by drawing a parallel between them and the Israelites whom Moses led out of Egypt. The Israelites had also been 'baptized', in a sense, as they passed through the water of the Red Sea, which God miraculously parted when they were being pursued by Pharaoh's army (10:1–2); and they had also received their equivalent of the Lord's Supper, the manna God gave from heaven and the water that was miraculously produced from a rock, which Paul calls 'spiritual food' and 'spiritual drink' (10:3–4). However, despite receiving these great spiritual blessings, 'God was not pleased with most of them' and judged them for their disobedience, so they did not enter the Promised Land: 'Their bodies were scattered over the desert' (10:5).

Paul is very concerned that the Corinthians should not miss the lessons of history. He stresses that 'these things occurred as examples to keep us from setting our hearts on evil things as they did' (10:6). The specific sins that he mentions all had their parallels in Corinth. The wicked behaviour of those who followed Moses' brother, Aaron, in worshipping a golden calf, was reflected in the idolatry of some of the Christians in Corinth who, it seems, took part in idolatrous festivals. The words Paul quotes from the account of Aaron's idolatry in Exodus 32 would have been very close to home: 'The people sat down to eat and drink and got up to indulge in pagan revelry' (1 Corinthians 10:7). They would have recognized some of their number also in Paul's reference to the terrible occasion in Numbers 25, when many Israelite men had sex with Moabite women and then agreed to join them in pagan sacrifices, which led to God sending a plague which killed 23,000 people in one day (1 Corinthians 10:8). It is likely that the prostitutes, whom a number of the men in the church visited (6:15–16), were based at pagan shrines. And the sin of testing the Lord (10:9) or grumbling, which included complaining against God's appointed leaders, Moses and Aaron (10:10), was also seen in Corinth where many in the church were turning against the God-given authority of the Apostle Paul.

'Be careful that you don't fall'

Paul concludes his history lesson by saying, 'These things happened to them as examples and were written down as warnings for us, on whom the fulfilment of the ages has come. So, if you think you are standing firm, be careful that you don't fall!' (10:11–12). The Corinthians had no reason to be complacent. They were engaging in exactly the same sins as those for which God had judged the Israelites severely. The implication was clear: they too could expect God's judgment unless they repented.

Some worry that the warning of verse 12 contradicts the precious doctrine known as the perseverance, or preservation, of the saints, which is drawn from wonderful promises such as the words of the Lord Jesus: 'Whoever comes to me I will never drive away' (John 6:37). That is to misunderstand Paul's intention.

The Bible has different messages for people in different spiritual states. It brings great comfort to those who are battling to live for Christ, but are finding it hard to do so, and assures them that 'he who began a good work in you will carry it on to completion until the day of Christ Jesus' (Philippians 1:6). Our security as Christians ultimately depends not on our feeble hold on Christ, but on his firm hold on us; he will not let us go. But there is a very different message for those who claim to be Christians and yet make no attempt to fight against sin. It is not good enough for them to say, 'I'm a Christian. I went forward at an evangelistic meeting ten years ago, so I've been forgiven, and God will never let me go.' The evidence of whether or not that was a genuine profession of faith will be seen not on a bit of paper they might have signed then, but in whether they are trusting in Christ and seeking to live in obedience to him today. The sign of past conversion is present convertedness, for the true believer keeps on believing.

'Flee from idolatry'

In 1 Corinthians 10:14–22, Paul applies his warning from history even more directly and stresses that the Corinthians must not have anything to do with pagan rituals. His basic point is expressed clearly in verse 20: 'The sacrifices of pagans are offered to demons, not to God, and I do not want you to be participants with demons.' It was true that an idol is nothing as there is only one God (8:4), but, although idols do not exist, behind them are demons, which certainly do. Involvement in sacrifices in pagan temples is therefore not spiritually neutral; it involves 'participation' or 'fellowship' with evil supernatural powers and, as such, should be unthinkable for a Christian.

Paul builds towards his conclusion by stating a truth he assumes the Corinthians already accept about the Lord's Supper, but which is not understood by all Christians today. As we take bread and wine, we are certainly recalling Christ's death for us in obedience to his command to 'do this in remembrance of me' (Luke 22:19), but we are not simply remembering him, we are also 'participating' in his body and blood (1 Corinthians 10:16). The word Paul uses speaks of a 'fellowship' or 'communion' we have with Christ. We do not simply look at the bread and wine as a means of being reminded of his sacrifice for us; we eat and drink them. They remain what they have always been, ordinary bread and wine, but, in the context of the Lord's Supper, they also symbolize Christ's body and blood. So, as we take them, we are, in the words of the old Church of England Prayer Book, 'feeding on him in our hearts by faith with thanksgiving'. As Charles Spurgeon put it, 'We not only eat of his bread but symbolically we feast upon him.'[5] Paul adds that we not only enjoy spiritual fellowship with Christ at the Lord's Supper, but also with all his people who are present: 'Because there is one loaf, we, who are many, are one body, for we all partake of the one loaf' (10:17).

Having established this truth about the Lord's Supper, Paul draws out its implications for those Corinthian Christians who attended meals in temples. Just as believers participate in Christ, so pagan worshippers participate with demons in their rituals (10:20). Christians who are present will thus also be drawn into fellowship with demons, an idea that horrifies Paul and should horrify the Corinthians as well. How could they think of having communion with the Lord at his table one day and then having communion with demons in a temple the next? Being involved in pagan sacrificial meals is not a legitimate expression of Christian freedom, but an outrage which must stop. The Corinthians were arousing the Lord's jealousy (10:22), which in Old Testament times often led him to judge his people for their idolatry. They were in grave spiritual danger and needed to repent.

The dangers of idolatry today

For some believers, such as those recently converted from other religious backgrounds, the issues raised in 1 Corinthians 10 are far from remote. Should they join with family and friends at a temple or mosque for weddings, funerals or other significant occasions? Those decisions are not easy and should be discussed, if possible, with other believers from a similar background. Some events may be spiritually neutral, but others may require, or imply, a level of spiritual involvement in what is occurring that is, at best, inappropriate for one who worships Christ as the only Lord. Refusal may cause offence and make it harder to build relational bridges for Christian witness, but there can be no compromise when spiritual integrity is at stake. The same principle will prevent Christians from taking part in inter-faith worship, where the Lord Jesus is worshipped alongside false gods.

The parallels for those from secular Western backgrounds may not be as obvious, but are no less real. We may not have eaten in pagan temples, but we are tempted to flirt with other kinds of idolatry. An idol is anything that we substitute for the one true God – Father, Son and Holy Spirit. It is, as Julian Hardyman puts it in his book on the subject, 'Anything or anyone we put in the place of God in our hearts – and therefore our lives'.[6] We may not be tempted to worship a metal idol in a temple, but we will be in danger of being drawn to live for the mental idols that our society values so highly: the gods of materialism (money and possessions), careerism, narcissism (health, fitness and beauty), eroticism (sex and relationships) and hedonism (pleasure). There is obviously nothing wrong with earning money, trying to do well at work, getting fit or having fun, but, when we begin to live for these things and they become more important to us than God, we are idolaters. They can get such a hook on us that there is a danger of us being drawn away from Christ altogether, and so we too, no less than the Corinthians, need to heed Paul's appeal: 'My dear friends, flee from idolatry' (10:14).

A young friend of mine once wrote to tell me why he had decided to stop being a Christian. He had begun to go out with a girl who did not share his faith and he had sensed the need to choose between her and Christ. He concluded, 'I cannot serve two gods; my girlfriend is my god.' Although I was very sad at his decision, I could at least admire his honesty and the clarity with which he understood what had happened. If we are to avoid spiritual shipwreck, we must have a similar clarity in recognizing the idols that threaten to take the place of Christ in our lives and, unlike my friend, take action to resist their pull. For example, one Christian whose spending was getting out of control cancelled a subscription to a magazine which fed her desire to buy things she did not need, and cut up her credit card. Another, who found himself beginning to live for his work above Christ, made a resolve never to work on Sundays or stay at the office late on

Wednesdays, so he could always attend a Bible study group at church.

Our particular challenges will vary. Some actions are forbidden for all Christians but others, where the Bible issues no clear command, will require judgment, as we consider what impact they might have on us spiritually. So, for example, Tom might feel that he is able to continue to go to pubs and clubs without being drawn back into his old sinful ways, but Simon decides to stay away because he fears the temptation will be too great. We must make our own decisions, taking care as we do so not to place ourselves deliberately into situations where we will find it hard to resist the pressure to conform to the world's ways. The compromises might be small at first but, if not addressed, they can lead a long way from Christ.

'Do it all for the glory of God'

Paul concludes his discussion of the issue of food sacrificed to idols by quoting a Corinthian catchphrase which we have already encountered: 'Everything is permissible' (6:12; 10:23). It is wonderfully true that we have great freedom as Christians and are not bound by the huge number of detailed laws which were such a feature of first-century Judaism. The Corinthians could eat anything they liked from the meat market 'without raising questions of conscience, for, "The earth is the Lord's, and everything in it"' (10:25–26), and they were also free to eat anything that an unbeliever served them (10:27). However, sometimes they should restrict the exercise of their freedom because, 'not everything is beneficial' or 'constructive' (10:23).

I hope we have discovered that these three chapters of 1 Corinthians, which, with their focus on meat sacrificed to idols, might have seemed largely irrelevant to us, in fact provide us with principles which help us determine how we should act in the large area of freedom in which the Bible gives no clear command. Those principles are summarized below, as well as in the flowchart for Christian decision-making on the next page. They were first described to me when I was a young Christian as 'The G Test', three Gs to consider before making a decision. They apply to small decisions, such as whether I should watch this film, buy that CD or go to a club, as well as bigger decisions, like how I should pass my leisure time or spend my money or even where I should live, whom I should marry or what job I should do.

The G Test

1. *What will be the effect on my spiritual Growth?*
   Will watching this film harm me spiritually?
2. *Will this be for the Good of others?*
   I might be able to watch the film without being harmed spiritually, but if my doing so might cause offence to a non-Christian, and thus make it harder to win him for Christ, or tempt a fellow believer to watch it as well, despite his conscience telling him not to, then I should not do so.
3. *Can I do this for the Glory of God? (10:31)*
   This consideration must trump all others. If I am not able to do something for God's glory, in a way that honours him, then it must be avoided.

Christian decision-making
(1 Corinthians 8 – 10)

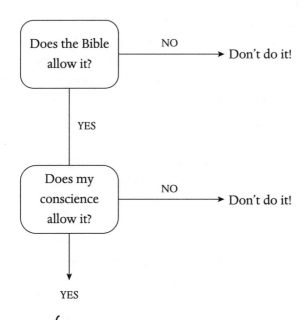

Does the Bible allow it? — NO → Don't do it!

YES

Does my conscience allow it? — NO → Don't do it!

YES

Area of freedom

Three further questions:

1. What is the effect on other Christians?
(Love is more important than knowledge.)

2. What is the effect on non-Christians?
(The gospel is more important than rights.)

3. What is the effect on my spiritual life?
(Spiritual health is more important than freedom.)

'DO IT ALL FOR THE GLORY OF GOD' (10:31)

Bible study (1 Corinthians 8 – 10)

8:1–13
1. Can you think of issues in our church life today which are equivalent to the Corinthians' differences over whether they could eat food sacrificed to idols?
2. What principles lie behind Paul's response?
3. How do they apply today?

9:1–27
4. Why does Paul not claim his right to be paid?
5. What would it mean for us to 'become all things to all men' (verse 22)?

10:1–22
6. What lessons is Paul teaching from Israel's history?
7. What do you need to do to 'flee from idolatry' (verse 14) today?

10:23 – 11:1
8. What priorities do these verses (and the whole passage) teach you that you should have when you make decisions?

Finally . . .
9. What have you learnt about true spirituality?
10. What alternative thinking does this challenge?

6. TRUE SPIRITUALITY
affirms gender differences, but not social divisions

(1 Corinthians 11)

'Fellowship with the Spirit'

I once met an older man who told me he was a Christian. When I asked him where he went to church, he replied rather curtly, 'I keep well clear of churches. My Christianity is between me and God and is no business of anyone else's.' That was an extreme expression of a common, but profoundly wrong, attitude. The Holy Spirit not only joins us to the Lord Jesus Christ, but also to other Christians, so that together we may experience 'fellowship with the Spirit' (Philippians 2:1). The presence of the Spirit in our lives has profound implications, not just for our vertical relationship with God, but also for our horizontal relationships with one another. This is one more area in which the indwelling Spirit should make us strikingly different from the world around us, although, sadly, we are often not nearly as distinct as we should be.

The relationships between the sexes and between members of different classes are potentially divisive areas in any age, so it is no surprise that they caused controversy in Corinth. In both cases Paul has to write to rebuke the Corinthians for their wrong thinking and behaviour. On the one hand, they had overstretched the radical implications of the gospel of Christ by diminishing the distinction between the sexes in a way that undermined God's creation purposes; on the other hand, they had failed to recognize the profound consequences of the gospel for how they related to those from other social backgrounds, and so the world's divisions were seen as much in the church as outside it. Paul's rebuke to the Corinthians will also challenge us; we too need to hear his message that true spirituality affirms gender differences, but not social divisions.

Gender differences (11:2-16)

The feminist revolution

John Gray's book, *Men Are from Mars, Women Are from Venus*,[1] one of the publishing sensations of the 1990s, has sold well over 7 million copies. According to one reviewer, the thesis that so grabbed its readers was simply 'that men and women are different'.

Feminism is undoubtedly one of the most significant cultural influences of the last century. The feminist movement has insisted that the non-biological differences between men and women are culturally determined, imposed by a patriarchal male-dominated society, and should therefore be resisted. Simone de Beauvoir, one of the founding sisters of feminism, expressed this view when she wrote, 'One is not born but rather becomes a woman.'[2] This movement has caused a dramatic social revolution that propelled women out of the private world of home and into the public sphere of work, education and politics, all within a few decades. Who would have thought in 1919, when Nancy Astor was elected the first female member of parliament in Britain, that just sixty years later we would have the first woman prime minister? It is hardly surprising that such a whirlwind of change has produced great confusion concerning sexual identity. There is no longer any consensus about what it means to be male or female.

Feminism has certainly achieved much progress, liberating many women from an overly restricted, narrow existence, but elements of its message have also led to disillusionment, as increasing numbers of women discover that the path of self-fulfilment and self-assertiveness often leads not to a brave new world, but to a sad and lonely one, and to exhaustion too. Being a 'superwoman'[3] sounds a great ideal, but is it *really* possible to juggle all the balls of family, career, hobbies and friends while still staying upright?

If women have been left exhausted in the wake of feminism, men are just confused. Young men, in particular, can feel emasculated by politically correct views, and while some adopt a metrosexual, almost asexual, identity, others assert their masculinity in aggressive, boorish ways. In the midst of all this confusion, it is as if John Gray tapped the shoulder of Western society and reminded us of the basic truth that men and women are different.

The Christian revolution

Nearly 2,000 years ago, another revolution took place. The consensus in Jewish society was clear: men were the superior sex and would even thank God daily in the synagogue for not making them women. No Jewish woman on her own would ever be spoken to directly by a rabbi and, although she could attend the synagogue, she had to sit apart from the men, not contributing in any way. But then came the revolution which was centred on Jesus of Nazareth.

Although Jesus never married and chose only male apostles, he accepted women in his band of followers, always treating them with the utmost respect and speaking to them like no other rabbi. Then, after his death and resurrection, the revolution continued in the life of the early church. The Apostle Paul is often dismissed as a misogynist, and yet it was he who said, 'There is neither Jew nor Greek, slave nor free, male nor female, for you are all one in Christ Jesus' (Galatians 3:28). He taught that men and women together had equal worth in the sight of God and were equal members in his kingdom. The change was also seen when Christians met together. The women were no longer segregated and they began to take an active role, which included praying and prophesying in church meetings (1 Corinthians 11:5). The changes were sudden and dramatic, so it is not surprising that they resulted in confusion, which led to some in Corinth taking the revolution too far. Paul writes in 11:2–16 to correct them.

A contentious issue

I am well aware that this topic of the relationship between men and women and their role in the church is highly contentious. As I write these words, the General Synod of the Church of England is engaged in heated debate over the proposed introduction of women bishops. Some speakers have referred to the embarrassment of belonging to a church which still bars women from the highest position of leadership and is, in their view, the last bastion of male chauvinism in a society that has rejected it. But the fact that our society holds a particular view is not a reason for Christians to adopt it. Sadly, there were very few references to the teaching of the Bible in the speeches at Synod, but surely the crucial question is not, 'What does our culture say?' but rather, 'What does God's word teach?'

Referring to this passage, David Jackman has written, 'Some passages are hard to understand, and so engage the mind at full stretch as we try to work out their meaning. Other passages are hard to accept, and so engage the will at full stretch as we try to respond to them in obedience. But this passage comes into both categories.'[4] I should acknowledge, before we try to grasp what Paul is saying, that there is much debate between Christians who accept the authority of the Scripture about how to understand both the details and the general thrust of these verses. This book is not the place for a long discussion of all the different views, so I will simply aim to outline what I think are the main points of Paul's argument. I am conscious that these issues can be very emotive and will try to tread carefully and not cause any unnecessary offence. I certainly make no claim to infallibility, so please do not take my word for anything I write, but rather study the Bible for yourself to see if you agree or not. Although it is hard to be certain about how to interpret many of the details, I contend that a study of this passage, and Paul's teaching on related subjects in other letters, can leave us confident about his basic message: that men and women are equal and yet different, having complementary roles.

'The head of the woman is the man'

Evidently some women in the Corinthian church had abandoned the customary head covering that was worn by women in those days, and did so because they thought the old distinctions between men and women had disappeared in Christ. Scholars debate whether Paul was referring to a veil, a shawl around the head or a kind of hairstyle, but we do not need to know the precise form it took in order to understand his argument. The apostle disagreed with their behaviour, because it failed to recognize that the fundamental differences between men and women, which go back to their creation, still remain since the coming of Christ's kingdom.

Paul teaches that 'the head of the woman is man' (11:3). The words translated 'woman' and 'man' can also mean 'wife' and 'husband', and it is likely that the apostle has the relationships within marriage especially in mind, although a wider application can also be drawn to the relationship between men and women in general.

There has been much debate about how the word translated 'head' should be understood. It was used mainly to refer to the physical head of a body, but was also used symbolically to speak either of someone in authority, just as we speak of the head of a school, or to refer to an origin or source, as we refer to the head of a river. There has been much debate as to which of these symbolic meanings Paul had in mind here. It has been increasingly common to argue that he is simply saying that man is the source of the woman, for she was made from man (Genesis 2:22), and that the expression does not imply that he has any authority over her. However, I suggest that Paul is not just reminding us of a fact of creation but assuming that it has present significance and determines the proper relationship between men and women. Man was not just the source, or origin, of the woman in the Garden of Eden, but is still the head of the woman now. That statement sounds shocking to modern ears and can easily be misunderstood and abused, so we need to take care to understand what Paul means.

On the occasions when Paul speaks of Christ as 'head', there is a clear implication of authority. In Ephesians 1:22 he states that 'God placed all things under his feet and appointed him to be head over everything', and there is a similarly strong statement in Colossians 1:18: 'He is the head of the body, the church; he is the beginning and the firstborn from among the dead, so that in everything he might have the supremacy.' In Ephesians 5 the same word is used to speak of the husband's role in relation to his wife, which is modelled on that between Christ and his church: 'For the husband is the head of the wife as Christ is the head of the church' (Ephesians 5:23).

Christian marriage

Just as the roles of Christ and the church are not interchangeable, so the roles of husband and wife are distinct. The wife is called to submit to her husband's headship, just as the church should submit to Christ (Ephesians 5:24). This does not imply that she is expected to be the lapdog of a brutal, domineering husband, always at his beck and call. She is her husband's equal in both creation (Genesis 1:27) and salvation (Galatians 3:28), and has no less dignity and worth than him. It will be entirely appropriate at times for her to disagree with him, and even plead with him to change his mind, but she should nonetheless acknowledge that the ultimate leadership in the relationship belongs with him. This is certainly not an excuse for him to abuse his position in a selfish and demeaning way. He is called to live up to the perfect, self-sacrificial example of Christ, and love his wife 'just as Christ loved the church and gave himself up for her to make her holy' (Ephesians 5:25–26). Christ is the perfect head who sets the standard for all human headship.

Christ's headship over Christians does not demean us, but rather enables us to flourish into the people that we long to be. He was so committed to our welfare that he was willing to go to the cross so that we might enter into the relationship with God for which we were made. In the same way, a wife will blossom if she is married to a husband who exercises his headship not to please himself, but in the interests of what is best for his wife, even if that kills him.

When I preach at weddings, I sometimes encourage the new husband to write down on his honeymoon the five qualities about his wife that he most admires, and then to consider them again every anniversary. If she is continuing to grow in these areas as the years go by, that is a sign that he is loving her as he should, but, if she is not, that may be a sign that he is failing to fulfil his role.

Men and women in the church

The distinction between men and women's roles is not limited to marriage, but is also reflected in Paul's teaching concerning the church, as in 1 Timothy 2:8–15. By not wearing their head coverings in church meetings and, at least in that way, making themselves look like men, a group of women in Corinth were effectively implying that the old differences had been abolished in Christ, but Paul disagrees. We are not simply people who happen to have male or female reproductive organs, but we are men and women. Our gender is not just a thin veneer spread over our bodies, but is much more fundamental. The non-biological differences between men and women are not all to do with culture and nurture, but have much to do with creation and nature, and therefore still apply in Christ's kingdom.

It is sometimes suggested that we should understand Paul's teaching in this area as simply reflective of his own first-century culture, and therefore as no longer applicable. However, he bases it not on arguments that are particular to his own era, but rather on the cross-cultural doctrines of creation and the Trinity. Referring to the account of Eve's creation in Genesis 2:22, he teaches that male leadership is a consequence of the fact that 'man did not come from woman, but woman from man' (1 Corinthians 11:8). The different roles of men and women are not therefore, in his view, just a result of the particular customs of his day, but rather part of God's creation design for humanity. They also reflect the different roles within the Trinity, in which 'the head of Christ is God' (11:3). That statement leaves no room for any suggestion that female acceptance of the headship of a man implies that she is inferior to him. The Son is equal to the Father in divine glory, and yet he gladly submits to his Father's headship and never rebels against his position, delighting to be the Son and to do his Father's will. His submission certainly does not imply any loss of value or dignity.

Paul concludes his complex argument with another puzzling statement: 'For this reason, and because of the angels, the woman ought to have a sign of authority on her head' (11:10). Nobody is sure why the angels are mentioned, although it may be that they are seen as the guardians of the created order. The word 'authority' has caused considerable discussion. The context seems to suggest we should translate Paul as saying that she should have a sign of submission to authority on her head; however, Paul does not explicitly state that, but rather says literally, 'she should have authority on her head'. The head covering seems, therefore, to be understood as a sign of her own authority. If so, it speaks not just of her submission to her husband, but also of her freedom as a woman to play an important role in the congregation. Her authority to do so is not by her seeking to become like a man, but rather by being a woman. God has made us different, with complementary roles, and we will most thrive and glorify him when we accept that distinction, rather than seeking to obliterate it.

Vive la différence!

One way we should express our acceptance of difference is by following the ways in which our culture distinguishes between the sexes. We should seek to avoid the kind of confusion that a friend of mine witnessed at a choral society. After everyone was asked to move into their appropriate group, one singer with flowing locks remained in the middle, so the conductor, assuming he was speaking to a woman, called out, 'Are you a soprano or an alto?' A rather wounded deep voice replied, 'I'm a bass!'

The head coverings and hairstyles that were familiar markers of masculinity and femininity in Corinth were particular cultural expressions of the creation differences. We in the twenty-first century are not bound by them, even if we could work out exactly what they were, but we should seek to conform to our own cultural equivalents so as to avoid any suggestion that we are seeking to rebel against God's design.

In Western culture, many clothes are regarded as being perfectly acceptable for both men and women, and there is no standard style in which the different sexes are expected to have their hair. However, some clothes are gender specific and certain hairstyles are normally associated with one sex. Christians will not want to transgress these cultural norms or in any way blur the distinction which is fundamental to who we are as human beings. We should rejoice in the fact that God has made us different as men and women, and resist the modern trend towards a bland and confused unisex society. As the French would say, 'Vive la différence!'

'Take my wife and let me be'

One obvious implication of Paul's teaching about male headship is that men should be willing to take a lead. The old joke that men turn the hymn 'Take my life and let it be' into 'Take my wife and let me be' is often much too close to the truth. At church prayer meetings, it is almost always women who pray first, usually because they have given up waiting for the few men who are there to open their mouths. There is, of course, no principle that men should speak first at a prayer meeting, but their reluctance to do so is just one symptom of an abdication of responsibility, which often leaves women feeling that they must fill the vacuum left by the failure of men to offer spiritual leadership in the home and at church. The husband should be the chief pastor in the home, taking prime responsibility for the spiritual teaching and care of his wife and children, and men should also be looking to take a lead in the church.

Women should encourage men in their leadership, but this certainly does not imply that they should be passive. As we will see, women were prominent in church life in the first century, although they did not serve as elders. Those who agree that men and women have complementary roles differ as to precisely what roles are appropriate for women to take. Rather than getting bogged down in discussions about particular roles, it will be more fruitful to keep the focus where the Bible places it: on the nature of the relationship between men and women.

Perhaps an illustration from my own, admittedly male, experience may help. When I served as curate in our church, I was conscious that the Rector was my boss. That meant that a few roles were inappropriate for me, such as chairing the Annual Meeting, which would have implied overall leadership of the church. It was, however, appropriate for me to engage in most areas of ministry, but, as I did so, I was always conscious that I served under him and I therefore tried not to do anything that might imply an undermining of his authority. So, for example, I knew I should never pronounce on some disputed matter of church policy without first referring to him. On a few occasions, when I led a Bible study with the Rector present, I did so slightly differently, deferring to him when I could and looking to him to have the last word in any discussion. Clearly there are differences in the relationships between a senior and assistant pastor, and between men and women, but there are parallels. Often men and women in marriage and the church will best discern what behaviour is appropriate for them not by looking for rules, but rather by remembering the nature of the relationship between them and then seeking to live accordingly.

The interdependence of male and female

Paul is anxious that nobody should misunderstand his teaching and conclude he teaches that women are utterly dependent on men, whereas men can flourish without women. Men have too often been guilty of an arrogant, patronizing chauvinism, which can claim no support from the apostle's teaching. He stresses that while it is true that 'woman is not independent of man', it is equally true that man is not 'independent of woman' (11:11) and that we depend on one another. Any man who is tempted to think that he does not need women should remember that he owes his existence to his mother (11:12). The interdependence of the sexes, which is seen so clearly in the natural order, also exists in the church.

Our church family at St Ebbe's is greatly enriched by the presence of women working alongside men on the staff team. It will obviously not be possible for every church to pay for women to work full-time, but it is important in every setting that we encourage and facilitate the active ministry of both men and women if God's people are to flourish. That certainly happened in the early church. The New Testament provides numerous examples of women making important contributions in a way that was revolutionary at the time. Although their testimony was still not accepted in court, the Lord Jesus chose women to be the first witnesses of his resurrection (John 20:1). A woman's home became the base for the earliest church (Acts 12:12), and Paul's first convert in Europe was a woman, Lydia (Acts 16:14). Paul mentions women frequently in his letters, not least in Romans 16 in which Tryphena and Tryphosa are two of as many as seven he names and are described as 'women who work hard in the Lord' (Romans 16:12). While some churches may be legitimately challenged to consider whether they are sufficiently reflecting the New Testament's teaching of the different roles of the sexes, others should consider whether they have allowed roles for women as prominent as that which they played in New Testament churches. These should not be simply behind the scenes, but also in more 'up-front' roles, such as those who prayed and prophesied at Corinth.

Social division (11:17–34)

'The history of class struggles'

Karl Marx and Friedrich Engels began their 'Manifesto of the Communist Party'[5] with the dramatic statement, 'The history of all hitherto existing society is the history of class struggles.' The great goal of communism was to put an end to such divisions and to produce a universal society of equals. That was in some ways a noble vision, but the attempt failed disastrously as the oppression of the aristocracy and bourgeoisie was replaced by the oppression of party officials. Whatever the theory, communism produced a society that was just as hierarchical as any that had gone before, as George Orwell brilliantly portrays in *Animal Farm*, in which 'All animals are equal but some animals are more equal than others.'[6]

Prejudice exists in every society, whether it is expressed in divisions between rich and poor, party members and non-party members, or those belonging to different races or tribes. It is distressing enough to see such division and discrimination in the world, but we should be especially outraged when it is found in a church. The Lord Jesus came to earth to call to himself a people from every tribe and nation, from all different backgrounds and every shade of colour to form one united family, his body the church, and what God has joined together we dare not divide. Yet Paul was horrified to hear that the world's divisions still remained in the church at Corinth.

Social divisions in the church

Paul begins this next section of his letter with a devastating statement: 'Your meetings do more harm than good' (11:17). The Corinthians' gatherings were so deeply flawed that it would have been better if they had stayed at home. The apostle spoke so strongly because he had received reports that, when they came together as a church, there were 'divisions' among them (11:18). It seems that he no longer has in mind the factionalism he countered in chapters 1 – 3 (for example, 1:12 and 3:4), in which groups allied themselves to the styles and personalities of different Christian leaders, but rather social divisions between rich and poor.

Paul has reminded the Corinthian Christians that not many of them were 'of noble birth' (1:26), but it is clear from 11:17–34 that they did come from a variety of social backgrounds. That in itself was certainly not a concern of Paul's; he delighted in the fact that the gospel of Christ was for everyone, rich and poor alike. What concerned Paul was not social differences between the Corinthian Christians in and of themselves, but rather the fact that they were allowed to affect how they related to one another. Instead of loving everyone as an equal member of the body of Christ, the rich Christians discriminated against their poorer brothers and sisters, and treated them differently. To make matters worse, this discrimination took place at the Lord's Supper, the very meal that was designed to symbolize their unity with Christ and with one another.

A terrible abuse

It was the custom of the Christians to eat a meal when they met together and, in that context, to share bread and wine in remembrance of Christ, as he had told his disciples to do. They assumed the Lord would approve of what they did, as he had instituted this practice, but Paul challenges their presumption, saying, 'When you come together, it is not the Lord's Supper you eat' (11:20). Their behaviour was so shocking that their meal could not be described as anything Jesus would recognize. Paul describes what was happening in verse 21: 'For as you eat, each of you goes ahead without waiting for anybody else. One remains hungry, another gets drunk.'

We cannot be sure exactly what form this behaviour took, but we can speculate. Sunday was a normal working day, so most Christians would only have been able to attend a church meeting after they could leave their work, but the wealthy would have been free to meet earlier. Perhaps they started eating and drinking as soon as they arrived, leaving the others to make do with the scraps that were all that was left by the time they joined the meal. Alternatively, it may have been that all provided their own food, and the rich indulged themselves with the first-century equivalent of caviar and fine wine, while the poor, sitting right next to them, ate their own meagre supplies. Some scholars suggest the rich and poor even ate in separate rooms. There were no special church buildings in the first century, so Christians depended on the hospitality of wealthy believers who would open up their homes. Archaeology tells us that the dining room in the kind of home that would have been used was fairly small and could fit only twelve guests at most, but the courtyard, or atrium, could seat between about thirty and fifty guests. It may have been, therefore, that the host invited his friends to join him in the dining room, where they could enjoy the sumptuous food he provided, while the rest of the church had to make do with the little they were offered, or had to provide for themselves in the atrium. As a result, they left hungry, while some of their fellow Christians rolled home, sated with the very best food and wine.

Whatever precise form their behaviour took, Paul is horrified and asks, 'Don't you have homes to eat and drink in?' (11:22). This question makes it clear that his target is the rich, who were the only ones able to afford their own homes. If they wanted to enjoy a private dinner party, they could have done so at home. To behave as they did at a church meal revealed a contemptuous attitude towards their fellow Christians and a willingness to 'humiliate those who have nothing' (11:22).

We may think that we would never behave in such an outrageous way, but we too, often without realizing it, can be guilty of discrimination within our churches. It is unlikely that the rich in Corinth deliberately humiliated the poor; they probably behaved unthinkingly, following the patterns of the world without challenging them by the standards of Christ's kingdom. In the same way, Christians today often reflect worldly prejudices in our relationships with other believers. We may know in our heads that we all belong to the same family in Christ, but we do not live out that truth in our behaviour. A new church member who is similar to us in race or background is likely to be welcomed warmly, invited round for meals and quickly integrated, whereas another who is different may be left largely unnoticed on the sidelines for weeks. That was the experience of many immigrants from the West Indies in the 1950s, who often found British churches so unwelcoming that they left and formed their own churches. Sadly, similar behaviour continues today, often unnoticed and unchallenged.

The Lord's Supper

Paul counters the discrimination by reminding the Corinthian church of the familiar words of Jesus as he instituted the Lord's Supper, so they might realize how far their meals had moved from his original intention. What should have been a time of serious remembrance of Christ's death and a celebration of their union with him, and with one another, had degenerated into a worldly excuse for self-indulgence. Paul should not have had to remind them that the Lord's Supper was meant to have the Lord at its centre: 'For whenever you eat this bread and drink this cup, you proclaim the Lord's death until he comes' (11:26).

The Lord's Supper is designed to proclaim not just the fact of Christ's death, but its significance. By dying for his people, the Lord Jesus made it possible for sinful human beings to be reconciled to God and thus to be a new humanity, united in him. We have already seen in 1 Corinthians 10 that some of the Corinthians did not live out the implications of their union with Christ, proclaimed at the Lord's Supper, and ate in pagan temples, thus having fellowship with demons. Now in chapter 11 we find that they are also not living out the implications of the other union which the Lord's Supper proclaims, namely that which they have with one another.

Paul reminded his readers in chapter 10 that the loaf which is broken and shared in the supper symbolizes the unity of Christ's people: 'Because there is one loaf, we, who are many, are one body, for we all partake of the one loaf' (10:17). All who trust in Christ are united with him and therefore with everyone else who is joined to him. This profound unity will be wonderfully revealed when Christ returns and all his people will be with him at 'the wedding supper of the lamb' (Revelation 19:9). That great occasion will be a wonderful declaration of the reconciling power of the cross, but meanwhile the Lord's Supper is to be an earthly reflection of that final manifestation of the Lord's people 'until he comes' (1 Corinthians 11:26).

This reminder of the nature of the supper Jesus instituted should have opened the Corinthians' eyes to the scandal of their behaviour. Jesus' death achieved a salvation in which social divisions had been broken down, and yet they dared to remember that death, as they took bread and wine, in a way that preserved those divisions. It is hardly surprising that Paul was so appalled and told them that it would have been better if they had not met at all.

'A man ought to examine himself'

Paul ends the chapter by drawing out the implications of the nature of the Lord's Supper for the Corinthians' behaviour when they met. He warns them, 'Whoever eats the bread or drinks the cup of the Lord in an unworthy manner will be guilty of sinning against the body and blood of the Lord' (11:27).

We should not misunderstand what Paul is saying and think he is warning us against approaching the Lord's table if our hearts are not completely pure. None of us can presume to come to the supper 'confident in our own righteousness'.[7] We all need to hear the encouragement that a Scottish pastor gave to a lady who hung back from receiving the bread and wine because she was so conscious of her sins: 'Take it woman; it's for sinners.' Paul's words in verse 27 are not designed to provoke an unhealthy internal search for sufficient worthiness, but to rebuke the behaviour of those, such as the Corinthians, who deny the reality of what Christ achieved on the cross by failing to live as one body in the church. This is a serious sin and places the Corinthians in the same category as those responsible for Christ's death rather than those who benefit from it. Until they repented, therefore, their participation in the supper did not bring them any spiritual benefit, but rather condemned them.

In the light of the solemn warning, Paul encourages the Corinthians to examine themselves before eating and drinking the bread and the wine (11:28), for if they do so 'without recognising the body of the Lord' (11:29), they will bring judgment on themselves. It has been suggested that the sin Paul has in mind is that of eating the bread and the wine as an ordinary meal, without focusing on the broken body and shed blood of the Lord Jesus, which they represent. However, it seems more likely that the 'body of the Lord' refers not to Christ's body on the cross, but rather to his body in terms of the church. Paul has already used the word in that sense in 10:17 and will do so again in 12:13. This view is supported by the fact that, in 11:29, Paul only speaks of the Lord's body and not also of his blood, and it is supported by the context as well.

Although it is undoubtedly true that we should reflect on the Lord's death when we take bread and wine, there is no indication that the Corinthians were failing to do so. Their sin was rather a failure to treat one another properly as they preserved the social distinctions of the world, even at the Lord's table. Rich Christians were failing to recognize the poor as fellow members of the body of Christ. That sin was so serious that it had already provoked the Lord's judgment and had led to the ill-health, and even death, of many church members (11:30). Paul encourages them to understand those serious events not as a final condemnation, but rather as the Lord's loving discipline through which he is warning them to repent (11:32).

'All one in Christ Jesus'

We also need to heed God's warning and repent of any attitude or action which undermines our unity as Christ's people. Every time we eat bread and wine together, we are not just remembering Christ's death, but are also proclaiming its fruits, which include the unity of all his people. The Lord's Supper, therefore, provides a good opportunity to examine ourselves and consider whether we treat one another in a way that is consistent with our unity in Christ. Social divisions are rife in the world but there is no place for them in the church. We may be a cabinet minister or a road sweeper, have three degrees or no qualifications, own two houses or be homeless, be Asian, African or European, but we are 'all one in Christ Jesus' (Galatians 3:28).

It has been said that:

- love for those who like us is ordinary
- love for those who are like us is narcissistic
- love for those who are unlike us is extraordinary
- love for those who dislike us is revolutionary.

Christ calls us to an extraordinary, revolutionary love that is different from anything seen in the world. Do our lives and our churches exhibit such radical love? Do we simply build relationships with those from similar backgrounds, or do we befriend others as well, even when that may be uncomfortable and draining? Do we seek to ensure that our church suits us and our type, or are we willing to sacrifice our own preferences so as to be as welcoming as possible to other Christians who are different? Is there any individual or group in our church who feels marginalized, or do all know that they are valued and loved? True Christian love will be costly, but it will also build a deeper, richer fellowship, which will not only enrich our lives but will also be a powerful witness to others.

'The final apologetic'

In his book about Christian work in universities around the world, Lindsay Brown describes a wonderful example of Christians living out the implications of the fact that we belong together in Christ. During a time of great tension in Burundi between the Hutus and the Tutsis, a number of Hutus were killed in tribal fighting on campus, which caused many Hutu students to flee to the mountains. Soon afterwards, Tutsi Christian students went to find them, taking food and clothing, first to their brothers and sisters in Christ, but also to others. As a result, some were rejected by their families, because they put their allegiance to other Christians above their allegiance to their tribe, but the non-Christian principal of the university said, 'Our culture is disintegrating. On our campus there are three types of people: Hutus, Tutsis and Christians. If our culture is to survive, we must follow the example of the Christians.'[8]

Politicians and revolutionaries have proved themselves incapable of removing social divisions, despite many attempts. The church should bear witness on earth to the miracle that will one day be perfectly fulfilled in the new creation: a wonderfully diverse community of equals completely united in Christ. Too often the world is repelled by our internal divisions and hypocrisy. If we would only begin to live out the implications of who we are in Christ, they would instead be profoundly attracted. As Jesus said, 'By this all men will know you are my disciples, if you love one another' (John 13:35).

Love is not just the distinctive mark of Christ's followers but is also 'the final apologetic'.[9] Non-believers will only take seriously the message of the cross if we live it out in our self-sacrificial, inclusive relationships with one another.

Bible study (1 Corinthians 11)

11:1–16

1. What does Paul mean by saying, 'The head of the woman is man' (verse 3)?
2. How does his reference to the relationship of Christ and his Father help us (verse 3)?
3. What does creation teach us (verses 8–9)?
4. What truth is taught in verses 11–12? How does this add to the picture?
5. How does Paul's teaching apply to church life?

11:17–34

6. What was going wrong in Corinth? How are you guilty in similar ways today?
7. Why does Paul remind the Corinthians of the nature of the Lord's Supper?
8. What more could you do to live out the implications of what it represents?
9. How would this change how you relate to Christians from different social backgrounds?

Finally . . .

10. What have you learnt about true spirituality?
11. What alternative thinking does this challenge?

7. TRUE SPIRITUALITY
prioritizes love, not spiritual gifts

(1 Corinthians 12 – 14)

Contemporary debates

Describing another church to me, a woman once said, 'You can tell they're a spiritual church – they're using all the gifts.' In particular, she had in mind a few gifts which have been brought into prominence in recent decades by the Charismatic Movement: tongues, prophecy and healing.

The Charismatic Movement, along with its sister movement, Pentecostalism, has had a remarkable impact throughout the world. There is considerable diversity of theology and practice among Charismatic Christians, but all are united in stressing the continuing use and significance of all the spiritual gifts mentioned in the Bible. There has been much debate and, sadly, sometimes division, about these issues. As a result, we are likely to have questions already in our minds, such as: What exactly are the gifts of tongues and prophecy? Are we still to expect in our church life all the gifts referred to in the New Testament? How many gifts are there?

These are important topics which, given the intense debate that surrounds them, I will try to address in what will be a longer chapter than the others. However, we should resist the temptation to deal straight away with our modern discussions and read 1 Corinthians 12 to 14 as if Paul wrote it directly to us to address our twenty-first-century questions. We should remember once more that, if we are to see what 1 Corinthians means today, we must first understand what it meant originally. That will involve trying to read between the lines to work out the situation to which Paul was responding in Corinth, and how he addressed it. Only when we have done that will we be in a position to apply the principles to our own questions and circumstances.

These chapters are corrective

It soon becomes clear that these chapters of 1 Corinthians are corrective. Paul was not trying to write the definitive guide to spiritual gifts, which would answer the questions of all Christians for all time, but was rather writing to correct wrong understanding and practice in a particular church 2,000 years ago. The problem Paul sought to tackle in Corinth was focused on the inflated value they attached to the gift of tongues. The word 'tongues' simply means 'languages'. It is unlikely that the practice Paul refers to involved the speaking of known languages of other people groups, as it had on the day of Pentecost described in Acts 2 when the Holy Spirit miraculously enabled the disciples to declare God's praises in languages they had not previously known. It is more likely that the tongues in Corinth were spiritual languages that no-one else could understand, even the speaker himself, unless God gave him the ability to interpret it. It seems that some regarded these special languages as evidence that they had arrived spiritually (4:8), and it may even have been that they thought they were angelic languages (13:1) and, as such, a clear sign of their exalted state. As a result, they regarded themselves as spiritually superior to those who did not have the gift of tongues and had therefore, in their view, not reached the same level of heavenly experience. In his response Paul is always positive about spiritual gifts, including the gift of tongues, but he challenges the way the Corinthians regard its presence and, no doubt, that of certain other gifts, as a key marker of true spirituality. Spiritual gifts are important, but, Paul insists, love is more important.

We will find that these chapters of 1 Corinthians leave some of our contemporary questions about spiritual gifts unanswered, but they will, however, present us with a powerful challenge. Our debates often focus on particular gifts, and whether certain Christians are overemphasizing or underemphasizing them. Whichever side we find ourselves on in these discussions, God's challenge to us is to focus above all not on the gifts, but on love. It is ironic that one of the areas in which we have most demonstrated our lack of love for other Christians has been our disagreements with them about the ministry of the Holy Spirit today. We have often caricatured and dismissed those who take a different view, and divided into factions, despite the point that very often we are in agreement with them on other fundamental issues such as the divinity of Christ, the necessity of the new birth, justification by faith alone and the authority of the Bible. We, no less than the Corinthians, need to be reminded that love is far more important than any particular view about the nature and use of tongues or prophecy. True spirituality prioritizes love, not spiritual gifts.

All Christians are spiritual

Paul begins this new section of the letter by saying, 'Now about spiritual gifts, brothers, I do not want you to be ignorant' (12:1). The word translated 'spiritual gifts' (*pneumatikoi*) is in fact different from the usual word Paul uses to describe gifts,[1] but is a more general word, which might be better translated as 'spiritual things' or 'spiritual people'. It is possible this was the word the Corinthians themselves used for the supernatural manifestations that they valued so much, or to describe those whom they believed belonged to a spiritually élite group. They prided themselves on their knowledge, not least on spiritual matters, but Paul humbles them by saying that they are in fact in danger of being 'ignorant' on the matter; the word means literally 'without knowledge'. After all, it was not long ago, when, before their conversion, they had been so ignorant spiritually, that they had been worshipping mute idols (12:2). They had been badly wrong before, and to avoid such spiritual ignorance again, they simply needed to understand one truth.

Our ears will surely prick up when we hear that Paul is about to tell us how to avoid being ignorant about spiritual things. Here is the apostle's foundational teaching about spirituality which it is vital that we grasp. What are we expecting? I doubt any of us would have anticipated the lesson that he does teach us, which at first reading, seems to be an anticlimax: 'That no-one who is speaking by the Spirit of God says, "Jesus be cursed," and no-one can say, "Jesus is Lord," except by the Holy Spirit' (12:3).

The basic lesson about spirituality is simply this: the spiritual person is any Christian who can say 'Jesus is Lord' and mean it. By nature, none of us will recognize the truth of Christ's unique identity as Saviour and Lord and respond to him with repentance and faith; that will only happen by the miraculous work of the Holy Spirit in our lives making us new people. It is only by the Spirit that we can be born again and cross from darkness to light and from spiritual death to spiritual life. This conversion, and the consequent acknowledgment of Christ's lordship, is the only marker that distinguishes a spiritual from an unspiritual person. All Christians are spiritual!

The unity of the Spirit

This foundational lesson was an important corrective for the super-spiritual group who spoke and acted as if there were two types of Christians in the church: spiritual and unspiritual. It is also a lesson that we urgently need to remember today. A great deal of confusion and hurt has been caused in recent decades by Christians overtly teaching, or at least implying, that they are spiritual and that other believers, although converted as well, are not. Many churches have split, and friendships have been greatly strained as a result. Let us pray that we will not make the same mistakes in the future. Some of our differences on the subject of spiritual gifts are significant and we should continue to discuss them, but we must not let them get out of proportion.

In Ephesians 4:3, Paul urges us to 'make every effort to keep the unity of the Spirit through the bond of peace'. He assumes that a profound spiritual unity already exists among Christians, not because we share the same views on every aspect on the nature and use of spiritual gifts, but, far more importantly, because the Holy Spirit has worked in our lives to join us to Christ and therefore to one another. We are already one in Christ and are now called to work out that unity in practice, not least by the patience, respect and love we show one another when we disagree on secondary matters.

1. Unity in diversity (1 Corinthians 12)

Spiritual gifts

The word Paul uses for spiritual gifts (*charisma*, verse 4) has the Greek word *charis*, meaning 'grace' or 'undeserved gift', as its root. We have seen that he uses it elsewhere to speak of any gift of God's grace, including singleness or marriage (7:7) and salvation (Romans 6:23), but here it refers to any God-given ability of a Christian which God uses to bless other believers. We very quickly feel proud and boast about our gifts, either openly or within the secrecy of our hearts. This is perverse when we remember that they are not something we have achieved, but have rather been given by God's grace, as the very word Paul uses to describe them emphasizes. Writing to a church that was prone, like us, to spiritual pride, he stresses repeatedly that the gifts are 'given' (1 Corinthians 12:7, 8, 11). Our response should therefore be one of gratitude, not pride. As Paul asked the Corinthians earlier in the letter, 'What do you have that you did not receive? And if you did receive it, why do you boast as though you did not?' (4:7).

One giver, different gifts

All Christian groups tend to consider the possessors of certain gifts as more highly spiritual than others, whether it is those who have the gifts of tongues, prophecy and healing, or of preaching, teaching and evangelism. Paul, however, stresses that all come from the same source. The gifts may be 'different' (12:4, 5, 6) but they are given by 'the same Spirit' (12:4), 'the same Lord' (12:5) and 'the same God' (12:6). His reference to the Holy Trinity is surely not accidental. Just as there is both unity and diversity within the Godhead, so there is unity and diversity within the church he has called.

Paul includes a list of some of the various gifts in verses 8–11, and again in verse 28. There are three other lists of gifts in the New Testament,[2] and it is striking that all of them differ from the others. Ten gifts are mentioned in this chapter, and a further ten elsewhere in the New Testament, but there is no reason to believe that there are only twenty gifts in all. Music and hospitality, for example, may not be described explicitly as spiritual gifts, but they surely belong to the same category, as does any means by which God ministers his grace through a believer to other Christians to build them up.

The variety of the gifts Paul mentions is noteworthy. No clear distinction is drawn between abilities we might consider rather mundane, for example, 'those able to help others' and 'those with gifts of administration' (12:28), and the more obviously supernatural gifts, such as the ability to work miracles (12:29). The gifts are not defined and it is often impossible to know exactly to what Paul is referring. What, for example, is a 'message of wisdom' (12:8)? We may speculate that it could be some kind of revelation, a wise saying, or even the proclamation of the cross, which is God's wisdom (1:24), but we cannot be sure. Anthony Thiselton devotes fifty-three pages in his commentary[3] to verses 8–11 alone, which averages out at about six pages for each gift, in which he outlines the different possible interpretations. We may presume that the Holy Spirit would have made it clearer to us if it was important that we knew the exact nature of every gift. Paul is not giving us a checklist against which we should measure our church to see if all the different gifts he mentions are present. He presumably refers to these particular gifts and not others because they were especially prevalent in Corinth or were the subject of controversy. We completely miss his thrust if we conclude from our study of this chapter that ours cannot be a spiritual church unless we see evidence of all the particular gifts Paul mentions in 1 Corinthians 12.

The gift of the bassoon

I have described elsewhere[4] an analogy which makes the point that Paul is not providing a blueprint in 1 Corinthians 12 that all churches should copy in every detail:

Suppose a church has many members who play the bassoon. They are proud about this and give the impression that all truly spiritual people should be bassoon players. They also think it is their right to exercise their gift when the church meets. They insist, 'God has given us our gift and we must use it.' The result is chaos: fifty people playing the bassoon at the same time. Paul writes to correct this abuse. He affirms the gift: 'I play the bassoon as much as any of you. It is a good gift to have. The church is helped to praise God when someone plays.' But then he criticizes them: 'We're meant to be different and not all have the same gifts – that way we function best. So please, could you limit yourselves to just two bassoonists each Sunday? And could some of you look to serve in other ways? How about learning another instrument or helping with the coffee after church, for example?'

What would be our reaction if we unearthed that letter after 2,000 years? Would we panic about the fact that no-one in our music group plays the bassoon and that we cannot therefore be a spiritual church? That would miss the point. There are hundreds of different gifts (means by which God can edify a congregation through the ability of one member). No church can conceivably manifest all the possible gifts at any one time. Paul does not expect us to. The point is not that a spiritual church will have bassoon players, but rather the principle that there is a great variety in the gifts God has given.

And he wants us to use those different gifts in the loving service of others.

One body, many parts

Paul introduces his own illustration to underline the point he stresses throughout the chapter that there is unity in diversity. He likens the local church to the human body, which is a unity and yet consists of many parts (12:12). In a similar way, he writes, 'We were all baptized by one Spirit into one body – whether Jews or Greeks, slave or free – and we were all given the one Spirit to drink' (12:13).

Contrary to those in Corinth who implied that only some Christians had received the Holy Spirit, Paul is in no doubt that all Christians have been 'baptized in the Holy Spirit'. This verse was important to me when I was going through the spiritual crisis that I referred to earlier, caused by those who suggested that, although I had trusted in Christ and been converted, the Holy Spirit was still outside my life. I found John Stott's book, *Baptism and Fullness*, especially helpful at that time, in particular his explanation of 1 Corinthians 12:13. This, he argues, shows that Paul regarded the baptism of the Holy Spirit not as an experience that only some Christians have received, but as conversion. He concludes, 'The gift of the Holy Spirit is a *universal* Christian experience because it is an *initial* Christian experience.'[5]

Baptism in the Spirit, or conversion, is the basis of our unity as Christians. We have all been joined to Christ and therefore to his body, the church, by the Holy Spirit, and so we belong together as one unit. However, just as there is diversity within the one human body because of the different parts of which it consists, so there is diversity within Christ's body, the church, because of the different gifts he has given to its members. Far from lamenting this diversity, as some in

Corinth did by wishing that all believers could have the same gift of tongues, we should rejoice in it, as it enables us to function well together.

'I don't belong'

Those in Corinth who did not belong to the group that regarded itself as spiritually élite were tempted to feel useless. Paul applies the image of the body to show them how wrong their thinking is. He writes, 'If the ear should say, "Because I am not an eye, I do not belong to the body," it would not for that reason cease to be part of the body. If the whole body were an eye, where would the sense of hearing be?' (12:16–17).

Paul's point was illustrated in a short story I once read which featured a human being who consisted simply of one massive eye. He had twenty-twenty vision but was, nonetheless, completely ineffective because he was unable to do anything in response to all that he saw. The eye may be an important part of the body, but it still needs the other parts. In the same way, God has not designed us to function on our own, for we need one another if we are to grow in the Christian life and be fully used in Christ's service. We should not lament the fact that we do not have other gifts, but rather play our full part in the body with whatever gifts we do have. Just as every part of the human body has a purpose, so every Christian has an important role to play in Christ's body, the church. That might be hard for us to believe sometimes, especially when we are feeling weak, but it is gloriously true.

I once visited a much-loved member of our church family when she was feeling very low. Daphne had suffered from depression for many years, and on this occasion it made her feel worthless, both to God and to the rest of the church. She insisted repeatedly, 'I'm useless; I'm no good to anyone.' I tried to persuade her that nothing could be further from the truth. None of us will know in this world how much we benefitted from her prayerfulness, but I often wonder how many of the blessings we received at St Ebbe's were as a result of God's answers to her persistent prayers. I know she prayed for me every day until she died, and the knowledge of that was a huge encouragement to me. I, along with many others, was also greatly helped by her frequent words of wisdom and her example of godliness in the face of great suffering. She did not have a visible, up-front role and she felt weak and insignificant, but her gifts were powerfully used. We too, however inadequate we may feel, have an important role to play. As Paul says, 'To *each one* the manifestation of the Spirit is given for the common good' (12:7).

'I don't need you'

While some Christians in Corinth felt inferior, others were proud. They thought they were the ones everyone else depended on and gave the impression to the rest of the church that they were superfluous. Again Paul uses the image of the body to point out their folly. Just as 'the eye cannot say to the hand, "I don't need you!"' (12:21), so no individual member of Christ's body can think they are self-sufficient.

This teaching is challenging in an individualistic generation which tends to keep all but a very few people at arm's length. We are so frenetic, spinning the plates in the different compartments of our lives, that we can easily lapse into regarding church as just one of many products we consume. I even read of a church in America that sought to meet such demands by offering a drive-in Sunday service which enabled people to tune into worship on their radio in the parking lot without getting out of their cars. We may be shocked by that, and yet the reality is that many Christians who do physically attend church meetings have little more interaction with other people there than if they had stayed in their cars outside. They rush in at the last minute and leave as soon as possible at the end, having had only the briefest of conversations with one or two others. Church is certainly not meant to be like that; we need one another.

The Christian community

No part of the human body can function unless it is attached to the rest of its parts and, in a similar way, individual Christians are not designed to function independently of a church. Most of the New Testament is addressed not to individuals, but to churches, and it is as a community that God expects us to grow together in the Christian life and be his witnesses in the world. It is therefore very important that we make finding a church a priority when we move into a new area, and do all we can to attend regularly.

However, we should not see church simply as a meeting we attend, but rather as a community to which we belong. That will mean working hard to build close relationships with others so that we can give and receive to the full. Our relationships should be so close that, just as in a body, 'if one part suffers, every part suffers with it' (12:26), so we feel the joys and sorrows of our Christian brothers and sisters. We will not be able to form such close bonds with every member if we belong to a larger church. In that case, committed membership of a small group is often very important, and it may well be in that context that we are most able to give to, and receive from, others more deeply. These relationships will take time to build, so it is important that we persevere. Instead of waiting for others, we should take the initiative. And it is almost always those who give most to others who also receive the most.

God has ensured that we are not the same, so that, when we serve one another in the church, we will contribute in different ways. Paul therefore concludes 1 Corinthians 12 with seven questions: 'Are all apostles? Are all prophets? Are all teachers? Do all work miracles? Do all have gifts of healing? Do all speak in tongues? Do all interpret?' (12:29–30). The answer is 'no' in every case. We must resist any suggestion by others that we should all have the same gifts, as some in Corinth were saying with regard to the gift of tongues, something which forms the climax to Paul's series of questions. We are not meant to be the same, but have rather been given different gifts by our gracious God so that we can function well together as one body. Instead of wishing that we had other gifts, we should use the ones we have received to do all we can to encourage and strengthen others.

2. Love is more important than gifts (1 Corinthians 13)

'The most excellent way'

The text of 1 Corinthians 13, with its beautiful description of love, is one of the most familiar chapters in the Bible. At first sight it may look out of place, as if Paul has misfiled one of his wedding sermons between two chapters about spiritual gifts, but in fact it is carefully written to communicate just what he needs to say at this stage of his argument and forms a bridge between chapters 12 and 14. If God has deliberately given a variety of gifts (chapter 12), then we need to exercise them for the good of the body and seek those that most build others up (chapter 14). What we need above all else is love (chapter 13), which Paul calls 'the most excellent way' (12:31).

The Corinthians were convinced that they were spiritual because of their gifts, but Paul wants them to understand that the chief mark of spirituality is not certain abilities, but love. He begins the chapter by mentioning again the gift that was most highly regarded by them and says, 'If I speak in the tongues of men and of angels, but have not love, I am only a resounding gong or a clanging cymbal' (13:1). We know from chapter 14 that it was common, when the church met, for some to speak in tongues, which no-one else understood, and Paul says there that, without interpretation, such speaking does no good to anyone except the speaker (14:7–11, 18–19). Such a use of the gift of tongues in a church meeting is unloving because it is not concerned with the effect it may have on others, and is of no more value to the church than the cacophony of sound that was a regular part of pagan worship, in which it was common for gongs and cymbals to be sounded so as to drive away demons and call the attention of the gods. Paul is saying, therefore, that spectacular phenomena in themselves are not a sign of God's presence and blessing. Our meetings can be full of remarkable supernatural happenings and yet, without love, they would be no different from mere paganism.

Indispensability

Love is not only more important than the gift of tongues, which the Corinthians valued so much, but also more important than the gifts that Paul most prized. He continues, 'If I have the gift of prophecy and can fathom all mysteries and all knowledge, and if I have a faith that can move mountains, but have not love, I am nothing' (13:2). I could preach brilliant sermons, lead outstanding Bible studies, know my Bible from cover to cover and be able to give confident answers to any theological question; I could understand God's ways deeply and be able to discern his message for every individual and situation; I might be so full of faith in God's power that I could move Mont Blanc to London; and yet, even then, without love I am nothing.

Paul really could not have made the point more strongly and yet still he has not finished. He says, 'If I give all I possess to the poor and surrender my body to the flames, but have not love, I gain nothing' (13:3). He is pointing to the most dramatic examples of personal sacrifice he can think of: a willingness to give up all possessions and life itself, and yet, even such dramatic acts have no value in the sight of God without love.

These powerful words were designed to challenge and confront the Corinthians' false view of spirituality. They were dazzled by outward actions and dramatic phenomena, but God looks at the heart. It is true that Paul does encourage the Corinthians to desire spiritual gifts, especially prophecy, in the next chapter, but first he wants them to seek love, without which the gifts are worthless. It is possible to be spiritual without having certain gifts, but it is not possible to be spiritual without love, which is indispensable.

Character

The words in verses 4–7 are perhaps the most familiar and have often made eyes moist at weddings, but Paul is not speaking of romantic love or the mutual affection of friends. The Greeks had words for both those emotions, but Paul uses a different word (*agapē*) for love here, which speaks not so much of an emotion, but an attitude that expresses itself in action. It is a settled disposition of mind, heart and will to do good to others, whether or not they have ever done good to us. The perfect model is the sacrificial love of Christ. As the Apostle John wrote, 'This is love: not that we loved God, but that he loved us and sent his Son as an atoning sacrifice for our sins' (1 John 4:10).

It has often been said that we have, in these verses from
1 Corinthians, a wonderful portrait of the love of Jesus. That
is undoubtedly true, but I doubt if Christ is in the forefront
of Paul's mind as he describes the qualities of love in this
paragraph. He is thinking above all of the Corinthians, and
he writes to shame them and reveal how far they have fallen
short of the standards of love that God demands.

Failure

Paul's readers should have squirmed as they read his description of love, because they had failed at every point. 'Love is
patient, love is kind' (13:4), and yet they were so impatient
that they were not even prepared to wait for the poorer
members to arrive before gorging themselves at their church
meals (11:21) and took no trouble to ensure that there was
anything left for the latecomers. Love 'does not envy, it does
not boast, it is not proud' (13:4), and yet some in Corinth
boasted in their gifts, their favourite leaders (4:6) and their
knowledge (8:1). Love 'is not rude, it is not self-seeking, it is
not easily angered, it keeps no record of wrongs' (13:5), and
yet the Corinthians insisted on their rights without regard to
the feelings of others, eating in idol temples despite the fact
that others in the church were scandalized by their behaviour
(8:10–12) and, far from burying the hatchet and making light
of wrongs, they even took one another to court (6:1). Whereas
'love does not delight in evil' (13:6), some in Corinth slept
with prostitutes (6:15–16) and were not shocked by the sexual
relationship of one of their members with his own stepmother (5:1–2). Unlike the Corinthians who lived for the
moment, love takes the long view and 'always protects, always
trusts, always hopes, always perseveres' (13:7). Love is aston-
ishingly resilient; it is not suspicious and cynical but seeks to
believe the best about others. It does not give up on people,

but is prepared to offer a second chance and to forgive even seventy times seven. Not only the Corinthians, but all of us, fall short when judged against the measure of this divine standard.

These words make uncomfortable reading for us today, no less than they did for the Corinthians. We share the Corinthians' obsession with power, knowledge and wisdom, and we too need to be reminded that, in God's view, none of these qualities count for anything if we are not loving. Before turning to another book for greater knowledge or attending one more conference as we seek spiritual power, let us first pray that the Holy Spirit would work in our hearts to produce the fruit of a Christ-like character. It is no accident that the first quality mentioned in Paul's list of the fruit of the Spirit in Galatians 5 is 'love' (Galatians 5:22).

Permanence

Paul concludes this wonderful chapter of 1 Corinthians about love by emphasizing that it is superior to spiritual gifts because, while they will one day cease to exist, love will remain for ever. The irony was that the very gifts which convinced the Corinthians they had reached the ultimate spiritual state would all one day pass away: 'Where there are prophecies, they will cease; where there are tongues, they will be stilled; where there is knowledge, it will pass away' (13:8). 'When perfection comes' (13:10), at the second coming, there will be no need for any more prophecies from God as we will then 'know fully'. There will be no need for spiritual gifts on that day, only 'faith, hope and love' will remain (13:13), of which love is the 'greatest', surely because it alone will continue for ever. Faith will in time be absorbed into sight, and hope will be finally and completely fulfilled, but love will go on and on into eternity because 'God is love' (1 John 4:16).

This magnificent chapter is a stinging rebuke to the Corinthians for their lack of love and an appeal to them to ensure that their approach to the understanding and use of spiritual gifts is driven by the priority of love and nothing else. We need the same message today, and Paul spells out what that means in practice in chapter 14.

3. The way of love (1 Corinthians 14)

Prophecy

In this chapter of 1 Corinthians, Paul applies the teaching of the previous chapter to the issues in hand. He begins, 'Follow the way of love and eagerly desire spiritual gifts, especially the gift of prophecy' (14:1).

There has been much debate about what is actually meant by 'prophecy' here. Bible-believing Christians have different views in this area, but those differences would, I believe, seem much less significant if we focus first on two truths that we should all be able to agree about: the Bible is sufficient and God is sovereign.

The Bible is sufficient

Whatever we may think about a continuing gift of prophecy today, we should be able to affirm that it is not on the same level as Scripture. The Bible is complete and sufficient: it tells us all we need to know God and live a life that pleases him.

Peter tells us that prophecy in the Old Testament 'never had its origin in the will of man, but men spoke from God as they were carried along by the Holy Spirit' (2 Peter 1:21). 'The Spirit of Christ' enabled them to predict 'the sufferings of Christ and the glories that would follow' (1 Peter 1:11). Now that Christ has come, we can expect no more prophecy of this kind, for, as the writer to the Hebrews says, it belongs to the past: 'In the past God spoke to our forefathers through the prophets at many times and in various ways, but in these last days he has spoken to us by his Son' (Hebrews 1:1–2).

Jesus, God's full and final revelation of himself, set apart the apostles to give us the authoritative record of his revelation. He promised that the Holy Spirit would both remind them of what he had taught them on earth (John 14:26) and also lead them into all truth (John 16:12–15). The New Testament is the fulfilment of that promise. Paul speaks of his fellow apostles, and possibly a wider group of other 'prophets' who were also entrusted with the revelation of the gospel in the first century, as the 'foundation' of the church (Ephesians 2:20). He says that this gospel 'was not made known to men in other generations as it has now been revealed by the Spirit to God's holy apostles and prophets' (Ephesians 3:5).

Now that the gospel has been revealed, and the foundation laid, there will be no more apostles and prophets of this kind. God's revelation of himself through Christ, as proclaimed in the Old and New Testaments, is complete. We are not to look for a new message, but rather to preserve, obey and proclaim what God has already said to us. Paul writes to Timothy, 'What you heard from me, keep as the pattern of sound teaching, with faith and love in Christ Jesus. Guard the good deposit that was entrusted to you' (2 Timothy 1:13–14). In a similar way, Jude urges his readers 'to contend for the faith that was once for all entrusted to the saints' (Jude 3).

The Bible is God's sufficient word for all time. It proclaims Jesus, who is God's final word, and his death on the cross for our sins, which is God's finished work of salvation. The Bible is all we need, not only to make us 'wise for salvation through faith in Christ Jesus' (2 Timothy 3:15), but also to guide us how to live a life that pleases God for, 'all Scripture is God-breathed and is useful for teaching, rebuking, correcting and training in righteousness, so that the man of God may be thoroughly equipped for every good work' (2 Timothy 3:16–17).

It follows from these truths that, if there is a continuing gift of prophecy today, it is certainly not on the same level as the prophecies of the Old and New Testaments. Our priority must always be to ask the Holy Spirit to help us understand and obey what we know is God's word, the Bible, rather than focusing on any other message, which we cannot be sure has come from God.

Prophecy in Corinth

Much of the discussion about prophecy in 1 Corinthians 14 focuses on whether Paul is describing foundational prophecy (what we might call 'capital P Prophecy'), the revelation of the gospel in the first century which will not be repeated in subsequent generations, or whether he is speaking of a different order of prophecy ('small p prophecy') which we can still expect today. I myself am not convinced by the 'cessationist' argument that there will be no prophecy of any kind after the completion of the canon of Scripture, but I do believe that prophecy will be of much less significance now than it was in Corinth.

When Paul wrote to the Corinthians, they only had the Old Testament Scriptures, as most of the New Testament had not yet been written. In those early days it seems that the church was especially dependent on the ministry of prophets, part of whose role was, by the inspiration of the Holy Spirit, to help them understand the Old Testament Scriptures in the light of Christ's coming and apply the gospel to their lives.

We tend to think of prophecy as containing a specific message from God for an individual or church which is especially applicable for their circumstances at the time (and

I do believe that this sometimes takes place), but that does not seem to have been the focus of the prophecy at Corinth which Paul describes in chapter 14. He tells us that prophecy 'strengthens, encourages and comforts' (14:3), 'instructs' (14:19) and 'converts' (14:24–25). Those sound very like the effects of the gospel and its application to today. The Corinthians did not have the benefit of a completed New Testament to teach them the fullness of the gospel and apply it to their lives. They were therefore especially dependent on the ministry of prophets, which may explain why Paul urges them to desire this gift above all others. It may also explain why, writing at the end of his life when 'the deposit' of apostolic teaching had all been revealed (2 Timothy 1:14), he places the emphasis not on prophecy, but on teaching, instructing Timothy, 'The things you have heard me say in the presence of many witnesses entrust to reliable men who will also be qualified to teach others' (2 Timothy 2:2), and urging him to 'Preach the Word; be prepared in season and out of season; correct, rebuke and encourage' (2 Timothy 4:2).

I am well aware that some readers will have a very different understanding of the nature of prophecy in Corinth from mine. That is inevitable, given that we have only a sketchy outline of what was happening there, and so we may have to agree to differ. However, whatever our differences, we should all be able to agree that the Bible is on a different level to any contemporary prophecy. We will therefore want to make sure that the proclamation and study of the Bible is central to our meetings. I was disturbed, after a few Christian gatherings I attended, when people seemed to be more excited about a claimed prophecy, which we cannot be absolutely sure is from God, than about the teaching of Scripture, which we can be in no doubt is God's living word for us today. The Bible alone is supreme and sufficient.

God is sovereign

On the other hand, some Christians are so concerned to stress the sufficiency of Scripture that they can give the impression that God's only involvement in our lives is when he is speaking to us directly through the Bible, as we study it ourselves and in groups, or hear it preached. The reality is, as cessationists would affirm along with many other Christians, that God is lovingly sovereign over every detail of our lives. When we meet together as a church, we are not like any other human institution, because God is with us. He is actively at work among us by his Holy Spirit, equipping each of us to play our part in building up the body, and he uses not just what we do, but also what we say, to that end.

The Spirit uses our words to edify one another in many different ways. He is certainly at work, enabling preachers not only to understand his word, but also to know how to apply it to our lives. At times we all have had the experience of feeling that the sermon was directed straight at us, as if the speaker knew the very situation we were in. That is not a coincidence; it is the sovereign God at work by his Spirit.

The Spirit is also at work in our Bible studies as he helps each member to contribute to the group's understanding of the passage and also to see how it impacts on their lives. And he is active in all our conversations when we seek to support one another and offer encouragement and advice. He is present too in every elders' or church council meeting, overruling what is said and equipping individuals to speak words of insight and wisdom about the direction the church should take. I can think of a few key meetings of our own council at which, with the benefit of hindsight, we can now all say with conviction that the Lord really used the words of a brother or sister to lead us to the decision we needed to take.

It could be argued that all of those instances are examples of prophecy (small p), especially if, like me, you hold to a broad definition of that term, which includes any means by which God uses the words of one believer to communicate, in the broadest sense, to others. The terminology is unimportant; what matters is that we make the most of every opportunity to build one another up with our words.

Unusual experiences

Most of the ministry of the Holy Spirit does not look especially dramatic or unusual, but there are occasions when he works in ways that are out of the ordinary. I have found, in talking to Christians who might be labelled as Charismatic, and others who are not, that both groups testify to similar experiences, even if they may use different language to describe them. Let me give a couple of examples from my own experience. There was the episode, for example, when, within a very short time, two friends of mine, both entirely unprompted by me and without consulting each other, gave identical advice which they could not have known was exactly what I needed to hear, or the occasion when I was (very unusually) given a deep conviction that a young woman, who had told me that she was very ill, was in fact perfectly well, even though there was nothing in her manner to suggest she was lying. Taking my life in my hands, and speaking as gently as could, I asked if she was sure she was unwell. She burst into tears, began to tell me what was really going on, and agreed to talk to an older woman who was able to share the gospel with her.

No doubt some Christians would label those instances as a prophecy or a word of knowledge. Others might not describe them in that way, but would still view them as evidence of the sovereign God at work. They too believe in a God who is actively involved in our lives. Once again, the labelling is unimportant, as long as we are clear if we use the word 'prophecy' for such occurrences that we are talking about what I call 'small p prophecy' and not the 'capital P Prophecy' we find only in the Bible. We can be absolutely sure that God's word in the Bible is completely true and authoritative, but we cannot have that same certainty about any other message we may feel he wants us to communicate. It is very unhelpful, therefore, if we introduce such a message with language such as, 'God is telling us . . .'. We should recognize that, however strongly we may feel that God is speaking to us, we may be wrong. It is only when we quote Scripture that we can say with authoritative conviction, 'God says'.

Practical implications

I have dwelt on these preliminary thoughts about the nature of prophecy because of the importance of stressing these two foundational principles. For some, the key challenge is to remember the supremacy of Scripture and not to allow an emphasis on prophecy to distract us from God's supreme word. For others, the challenge will be to remember the sovereignty of God and his active, intimate involvement in our lives by the Holy Spirit in many different ways. We should continue to bear these points in mind as we look briefly at 1 Corinthians 14 in more detail. We can summarize the very practical points Paul makes as follows:

1. Seek gifts that most enable you to build up Christians (14:1–19).
2. Seek gifts that most enable you to reach out to non-Christians (14:20–25).
3. Exercise gifts in a way that most builds up the church (14:26–35).

1. Seek gifts that most enable you to build up Christians (14:1-19)

Chapter 13 of 1 Corinthians is framed by the appeal of the end of chapter 12 to 'eagerly desire the greater gifts' (12:31), and a parallel instruction at the beginning of chapter 14 to 'follow the way of love and eagerly desire spiritual gifts, especially the gift of prophecy' (14:1). This is not a contradiction of the message of chapter 12 that Christians are given different gifts, but rather a recognition that, while all gifts have an important part to play, some have a bigger impact on building up the church than others. If Christians are driven by love, therefore, they will long to receive and develop the gifts that enable them most to edify others; this is 'the most excellent way' of love (12:31). In particular, Paul stresses that it will mean that the Corinthians will not value the gift of tongues above all other gifts, as they seemed to do, because it is of little use to others, but rather prophecy, which is a great help to the church.

Verses 1–19 are an extended comparison of the gifts of tongues and prophecy, in which Paul explains why the Corinthians should value prophecy much higher. The essential difference between the two gifts is summarized in verse 4 when Paul writes, 'He who speaks in a tongue edifies himself, but he who prophesies edifies the church.' Tongues is a private communication between an individual and God, perhaps expressing deep prayerful yearnings or feelings of praise prompted by the Spirit (14:16a). The practice can certainly be helpful to the speaker, and Paul testifies that he himself speaks in tongues often (14:18). However, he points out that speaking in tongues is only valuable for the individual and not for others, as they cannot understand what he is saying (14:2). Given that the church meeting is designed not for members to show off their gifts, but rather as a means of mutual edification, the Corinthians should refrain from speaking in tongues in that context unless what is said is 'interpreted' (14:13, 27–28) so that others can understand it, otherwise nobody benefits. The way of love means trying to 'excel in gifts that build up the church' (14:12), and that must mean a preference for prophecy over tongues, because prophecy is delivered in intelligible language.

The principle is surely clear, whatever our understanding of prophecy. We should long for the gifts that most enable us to build up other believers, and that must mean, above all, the ability to communicate intelligibly to them in a spiritually edifying way. We should look for every opportunity to speak to others for their 'strengthening, encouragement and comfort' (verse 3) and to 'instruct' them (verse 19). For some who are especially gifted, that will lead to a lifetime of preaching and teaching, for others, to studying the Scriptures and seeking training to equip them to lead Bible studies, Sunday schools and youth groups. For all of us, it will involve looking for any opportunity to spur on our fellow Christians.

2. Seek gifts that most enable you to reach out to non-Christians (14:20–26)

Prophecy is not just directed at Christians, but is also a means by which God communicates with unbelievers. We read in Revelation 19:10 that 'the testimony of Jesus is the spirit of prophecy' and so we are prophesying whenever we tell others about him. Paul has non-Christians especially in mind in this next section of chapter 14.

Paul once again warns the Corinthians, who prided themselves on their spiritual maturity, that they were in danger of being childish. In particular he regards their prizing of uninterpreted tongues, which nobody could understand, as a sign of immaturity. To make the point he quotes from Isaiah 28, in which the prophet spoke of the experience of God's people hearing unintelligible foreign languages as a sign of the fact that they were under God's judgment (1 Corinthians 14:21). That was because it would indicate that the country had been invaded by foreigners, as for example the sound of German everywhere on the streets of London in 1940 would have done.

Paul concludes, therefore, that since in Scripture when God's people hear unintelligible languages it speaks of God's judgment against their unbelief, tongues without interpretation in a public gathering should not be regarded as a sign of spirituality, but rather appropriate only for unbelievers. This is why he says in verse 22 that 'tongues, then, are a sign, not for believers but for unbelievers'. 'Prophecy', however, 'is for believers' (14:22), as it can be used to build up those who are already Christians and bring to faith those who are not. If unbelievers hear people speaking in tongues, they will be left confused and think they are out of their mind (14:23). If, however, they hear prophecy, a message from God in intelligible speech, they may be convinced of sin and even converted.

The way of love, therefore, means not just looking for every opportunity to speak so as to build up believers, but also to share the gospel with those who do not know Christ. Even in a chapter focusing on the church, Paul the evangelist cannot resist an application that encourages Christians to be concerned for the lost. We are not to look to the Holy Spirit simply to meet our own needs so that we feel contented and at peace, but rather to equip us to reach out to others. The Spirit was given on the Day of Pentecost to empower the church for the great task of taking the gospel to the ends of the earth (Acts 1:8), and the first thing Peter did, having been filled with the Spirit, was to preach the gospel to unbelievers. If we are driven by 'the most excellent way of love' (12:31), we will be deeply moved by the plight of those who do not know Christ, both in our neighbourhoods and on the other side of the world, and pray for the Spirit to equip us to play our part in reaching them.

3. Exercise gifts in the way that most builds up the church (14:26–35)

Paul now shifts his focus away from teaching about which gifts the Corinthians should most seek, to how love demands they should be used. The impression is that the church gatherings at Corinth were chaotic, with lots of people all trying to speak at once in a way that made it difficult for anyone to benefit. Paul has to remind them that 'God is not a God of disorder but of peace' (14:33), which means that their meetings should be orderly.

The apostle assumes that every member will arrive looking for opportunities not just to receive, but also to contribute encouragement in some way (14:26). However, love demands not only a readiness to use one's gifts, but often a willingness not to do so. To ensure maximum edification, many will need to keep quiet and resist using their gifts, so that everyone can gain from the words of whoever may be speaking at the time. Paul limits the number of contributions, for example, stipulating that no more than two or three prophets should speak (14:29), as any more would presumably strain the patience of the listeners and make it harder for them to benefit.

We should not understand these verses as providing us with a blueprint that must be applied to all Christian meetings. We should take the principles, not necessarily the details, of Paul's teaching here and seek to ensure that all that is done is in an orderly way and with maximum benefit to the greatest number. A smaller gathering, such as a house fellowship, the usual context for a church meeting in Corinth, is especially suitable for spontaneous contributions. Larger meetings are likely to require more structure, and love will demand that most of those attending will therefore remain silent, so that everyone can gain from the ministry of the few who do speak. It will be especially important for leaders of larger churches to encourage and provide for other contexts, such as smaller fellowship groups, where more people will be able to contribute.

In a puzzling verse, Paul teaches that 'Women should remain silent in the churches' (14:34). He cannot mean that they should not open their mouths at all, as that would contradict what he has said in chapter 11 where he approves of women praying and prophesying in the church meeting (11:5). It is perhaps more likely that Paul is forbidding women from being involved in the particular activity of weighing prophecies, which has been his focus immediately before verse 34. If so, Paul regards this activity as belonging to the leadership and therefore inappropriate for women, as it would be a breach of the principle of male headship. If the women had questions about any of the prophecies they should ask their husbands at home, rather than getting involved in the weighing process at the church meeting (14:35).

True spirituality submits to Scripture (14:36–40)

As he draws the discussion to a close Paul raises the question of authority, which is very important in any difference of opinion. Where should we turn in order to settle a dispute about the nature of true spirituality? The Corinthians, it seems, were content to look only to their own experience and collective judgment, according to which they concluded that they were authentically spiritual and, where he differed from them, that the Apostle Paul was not. Paul disagrees and calls on them to submit to the twin authorities of tradition and Scripture. These still remain today as the standard against which we must judge any claim to spirituality, with Scripture being the supreme test.

'Tradition' may be defined as the commonly accepted practice of believers down the ages and throughout the world. Paul had a high view of tradition and chides the Corinthians for their willingness to depart from it, both in the matter of women's head coverings in chapter 11, where he writes, 'we have no other practice – nor do the churches of God' (11:16), and concerning women's involvement in church meetings where he urges them to follow the practice of 'all the congregations of the saints' (14:33b). This principle has a wide application and should mean that we proceed with great caution before adopting any form of teaching or behaviour that diverges from the commonly accepted norm among Bible-believing Christians.

But while tradition is important, Scripture is the supreme authority. Nobody can claim that what they say or do is spiritual if it contradicts the teaching of the Bible, as Paul stresses at the end of this chapter. He challenges the Corinthians and says, 'If anybody thinks he is a prophet or spiritually gifted, let him acknowledge that what I am writing to you is the Lord's command' (14:37). Those who are truly spiritual will not resist Paul's teaching, as the Corinthians did, but rather accept him as the authoritative apostle of Christ and submit to what he says. That is an important principle for us to remember in an age when many professing Christians try to drive a wedge between the Lord Jesus and Paul, and think nothing of dismissing some of the apostle's teaching as no longer binding on us.

Paul leaves us with the particular challenge to repent of our selfish attitude to spiritual gifts and seek to follow the way of love that he has expounded. We are to resist the influence of our self-obsessed culture and instead live in a way that puts others first, doing all we can to strengthen our fellow Christians and reach unbelievers for Christ.

Bible study (1 Corinthians 12 – 14)

12:1–31

1. How would you summarize Paul's teaching in this chapter?
2. How does it change your attitude to spiritual gifts?
3. What does he say to us if we think:
   - 'I do not belong to the body' (verse 15)?
   - 'I don't need you' (verse 21)?

13:1–13

4. Why does Paul include this teaching about love here?
5. How does it challenge us?

14:1–40

6. How should 'the way of love' (verse 1) influence our attitude to spiritual gifts?
7. Why should we 'desire . . . especially the gift of prophecy' (verse 1)?
8. What might that mean for us?

Finally . . .

9. What have you learnt about true spirituality?
10. What alternative thinking does this challenge?

8. TRUE SPIRITUALITY
focuses on a physical future, not just the spiritual present

(1 Corinthians 15)

What happens when we die?

When the former deputy Prime Minister, Michael Heseltine, was asked in an interview if he was religious he replied, 'I think I'd describe myself as a prepared-to-be-convinced agnostic.' The journalist probed further, wanting to know what might convert him, to which Heseltine said in a classic politician's phrase, 'A more imminent approach of the central issues.' 'Is that what you call death?' asked the journalist. 'That's what I was thinking of,' replied Heseltine. 'That is a central issue.'

He is right of course; one day we will all die, unless the Lord Jesus returns first, and we would be foolish not to consider what will happen next. Thomas Hobbes, the philosopher, was prepared to acknowledge his ignorance, saying, 'When I die, the worms will devour my body and I will commit myself to the great "perhaps".' As far as he was concerned, everything was guesswork except the fact of the body's decay. Others are not even prepared to acknowledge the possibility of a continuing existence, holding along with Aristotle that 'death is a dreadful thing, for it is the end'.

Many find the thought of obliteration too depressing and choose instead to cling to some belief in an ongoing existence, perhaps through reincarnation, even though they are aware of no evidence for it. It is no wonder that people today are so uncomfortable when thinking about the future. It is not possible to escape death and the awkward questions it poses, and yet many have no answers in the face of it. Into this anxious confusion the Christian gospel rings out a glorious message of certain hope. Christ is risen! Death is defeated! All those who trust in Christ have a wonderful future to anticipate. Because Christ has been raised from the dead, we too will one day be raised and live with him for ever in a perfect renewed creation.

'No resurrection of the dead'?

Some in Corinth did not understand the implications of the gospel for the Christian's future and were even saying, 'There is no resurrection of the dead' (15:12). As we have seen already, they had a low view of the body, thinking that God was only interested in the soul or spirit. It was inconceivable to them that God's salvation would encompass their physical bodies. They believed they had already been raised and were enjoying the fullness of salvation in their spiritual lives, as witnessed, so they thought, by their ability to speak in heavenly languages. As a result, they focused entirely on the present, because, in their view, there was nothing significant to look forward to in the future except the shedding of their bodies at death, after which their spiritual life would continue as before.

This low view of the body, overinflated understanding of their present state and lack of interest in the future was at the heart of the Corinthians' wrong understanding of spirituality. It lay behind their proud boast that, now they had entered the ultimate spiritual state, they had left Paul and other ordinary believers behind. It also caused the contrasting problems of sexual immorality, justified on the grounds that the body was spiritually irrelevant, and asceticism, which argued that spiritual people should not lower themselves by engaging in a bodily activity like sexual intercourse. Their faulty theology explains their selfish insistence on their rights as well. As those who had been raised to the highest plane of spiritual life and experience, they were determined to enjoy it to the full, exercising their freedom and expressing their gifts, regardless of the effect on others.

The Corinthians thought they had already arrived, but, far from having reached the ultimate state of salvation, they were in danger of missing out on it altogether. Their denial of a future bodily resurrection was not just a minor flaw in their thinking, but a rejection of the gospel itself. We must not miss the sting in the tail of the first two verses of 1 Corinthians 15. The apostle is not simply reminding the Corinthians of basic gospel truths, he is also warning them of the spiritual danger they are in. They can only look forward to final salvation if they 'hold firmly to the word' Paul preached to them; otherwise they have 'believed in vain' (15:2).

A generation that lives for the moment

Paul's corrective in 1 Corinthians 15 is also much needed by us twenty-first-century Christians who often exhibit Corinthian tendencies in our thinking. We too can have a much lower view of the body than the Bible, as, for example, when leaders justify a refusal to exercise church discipline over continued sexual sin by saying, 'God is not interested in what we do with our bodies in the privacy of our own homes.' There is a tendency to focus more on maximizing our spiritual experience in the present than on the need for selfless, sacrificial holy living, as we keep our eyes on the glorious future to come. Teaching which promises material and spiritual prosperity now is much more attractive to us than any reminder that, wonderful as the blessings God has already given us in Christ undoubtedly are, the Christian life in this present world still requires self-discipline and suffering. Talk of discipline is not popular in a self-indulgent world which always tends to opt for the easy life; and teaching that points us to the future leaves many cold in a generation that lives for the moment and is frustrated by having to wait even a few seconds for an Internet connection. This chapter, 1 Corinthians 15, is therefore very much a chapter for our generation. It reminds us that true spirituality focuses on a physical future, not just the spiritual present.

'If there is no resurrection of the dead . . . '

In verse 12, Paul assumes that the Corinthians share his conviction that Christ himself rose from the dead, and on that basis seeks to point out the illogicality of their denial of any physical resurrection for Christians. His reminder of the basic truths of the gospel in verses 1–11, and especially of the fact of Christ's resurrection, is therefore not an attempt to convince them of what they do not already believe, but rather a re-establishment of common ground. He focuses on three fundamental facts: that Christ died for our sins, was buried and then rose again (15:3–4). Belief in the resurrection is not founded on mere wishful thinking, but on solid historical evidence. The risen Christ appeared to a variety of people, including on one occasion 500 Christians, of whom Paul says, 'Most are still living, though some have fallen asleep' (15:6). The implication is that if anyone doubts what he is saying, they could check the facts with those eyewitnesses who are still alive. Paul includes himself among them as one who met the risen Christ on the road to Damascus (15:8).

The fact of Christ's resurrection is the basis of the Christian belief that all who trust in him will also be raised. This is a fundamental tenet of the Christian gospel on which a great deal rests. Paul therefore tries to convince the Corinthians to reject their conviction that God will not raise us bodily by pointing out the terrible consequences of that view. Paul writes, 'If there is no resurrection of the dead, then not even Christ has been raised. And if Christ has not been raised, our preaching is useless and so is your faith' (15:13–14). Without the foundational belief of the resurrection of believers, the whole edifice of the Christian faith falls down.

The word translated 'useless' literally means 'empty'. If Christ did not rise, then Paul's preaching is baseless and without content, because it is robbed of one of its foundations, and the Corinthians' 'faith is futile' too (15:17), as they have been believing a lie. As a result, their convictions that their sins have been forgiven through Christ and that death is not the end for departed believers are both groundless: they are 'still in [their] sins' (15:17) and those 'who have fallen asleep in Christ are lost' (15:18). If there is no bodily resurrection, therefore, the Christian gospel is robbed of both its content and the comfort it offers: there is no faith, no forgiveness and no future. It is no wonder that Paul concludes, 'If only for this life we have hope in Christ, we are to be pitied more than all men' (15:19).

Firstfruits

The gloomy logic of verses 12–19 is interrupted by the great 'but' of verse 20. We need not despair, because 'Christ has indeed been raised from the dead, the firstfruits of those who have fallen asleep' (15:20). The 'firstfruits' of the harvest are the first pickings of the crop, which bring such encouragement to the farmer because they tell him that the full harvest is coming. The resurrection proclaims a similarly encouraging message: Christ is the first of many to be raised bodily after death. Death for the Christian is no longer to be feared, but can be compared to sleep, from which we will one day be woken to receive a resurrection body, just as Christ did. Christianity invented a new word for graveyards, 'cemetery', which derives from the Greek word for dormitory.

Paul's conviction that the resurrection of Christ was not an isolated incident is based on the fact that Christ is not simply an ordinary individual, but is the head of a new kind of humanity, so that what he does has repercussions for many others. The apostle explains this by comparing Christ with Adam, making the point that 'as in Adam all die, so in Christ all will be made alive' (15:22).

Adam was one man, and yet, as a result of his sin, death (the penalty for sin) entered the world and has been experienced by all his descendants ever since, because we are bound up with him and are 'in Adam'. When Christ, the divine Son of God, was born on earth, however, he was not 'in Adam'. He was a different kind of human being, not tainted by sin and therefore not deserving the penalty of death. However, on the cross he was willing to die for others, after which he rose again as the firstborn of a new humanity, no longer under the condemnation of death but able to enjoy eternal life in relationship with God his Father. Just as all are in Adam by birth and so face the terrible consequences of his sin, now Christians are in Christ by faith and, being joined to him, can therefore enjoy the wonderful fruit of his act of righteousness. This means we can be sure that, just as he was raised bodily, so 'those who belong to him' will be raised 'when he comes' at the end of time (15:23).

New creation

This truth that Christians will be raised bodily is as far as we tend to go in pointing out the consequences of Christ's resurrection, but Paul has a much broader vision. To grasp it we must understand that sin had terrible consequences, not just for human beings, but for the whole created order. God placed Adam and Eve as the rulers of his creation under him. When they sinned, therefore, the whole natural world was spoilt and was 'subjected to frustration' (Romans 8:20) and was in 'bondage to decay' (Romans 8:21). God, the great Creator, is determined to put that right, so his plan of salvation through Christ encompasses not just human beings, but everything that he has made.

Christ's death on the cross dealt with the problem of sin and, when he returns at the end of time, he will finally banish all its consequences. He will re-establish the kingdom of God and put everything right again. On that day he will hand over 'the kingdom to God the Father after he has destroyed all dominion, authority and power' which had been opposed to him (15:24). Although the decisive victory was won by Christ on the cross, his enemies have not yet admitted defeat and continue to fight a rearguard action, but their ultimate destruction is not in doubt, and one day even 'the last enemy', death, will be finally obliterated (15:26). Then, at last, God's salvation will be complete, and Christ, the king of the universe who has restored the order that was lost at the fall, will hand the fruits of his victory to his Father. At that time the one to whom everything has submitted will submit himself to his heavenly Father 'so that God may be all in all' (15:28), for, as we saw in 1 Corinthians 11:3, there is submission within the equality of the Godhead.

The resurrection should therefore greatly expand our understanding of salvation. God is not just interested in our souls, or even our bodies, but in the whole universe. He has demonstrated his commitment to the material world by raising Jesus bodily from the dead. His resurrection is a guarantee not just of our own resurrection, but of the restoration of all things. Our destiny is not a heavenly realm which bears no relation to the world we live in, but rather a perfectly restored creation in which everything has been put right, under the lordship of Christ. C. S. Lewis describes this truth vividly when he writes of the resurrection, 'He [Christ] has forced open a door that has been locked since the death of the first man. He has met, fought and beaten the King of Death. Everything is different because He has done so. This is the beginning of the new creation: a new chapter in cosmic history has opened.'[1]

Two ways to live

Whether or not we believe Paul's vision of the future has significant practical consequences for how we live now. He invites us to imagine the implications if there is no future resurrection. His statement in verse 29 is notoriously hard to understand: 'If there is no resurrection, what will those do who are baptised for the dead? If the dead are not raised at all, why are people baptised for them?' Many different possible interpretations have been suggested, none of which has convinced everyone. If, as at least a surface reading of the verse suggests, some in Corinth were being baptized on behalf of others, perhaps friends or relatives who had already died, Paul cannot have approved of the practice, as he stresses throughout his teaching that we must all make our own response to Christ. His point, however, is not to approve or disapprove of whatever he is referring to, but rather to point out that it would make no sense unless the dead are raised.

Paul points out that his own lifestyle would also be rendered foolish if there was no hope of a bodily resurrection. In that case, instead of submitting himself to great danger (15:30), the risk of death (15:31) or, on one occasion, being forced to fight with wild animals (15:32) for the sake of the gospel, he would surely have been wiser to live self-indulgently and agree with those who said, 'Let us eat and drink, for tomorrow we die' (15:32).

Those words are a sad summary of the philosophy of many whose lives consist of the pursuit of maximum pleasure now. They do not fear a future judgment or have the hope of a perfect new creation to look forward to, so they do all they can to accumulate possessions and experiences in this world without a thought for God and his standards. If Christians allow themselves to be influenced by those who undermine the truth of the resurrection, they too will begin to descend into such hedonism, even if it appears in a spiritually respectable form, and will avoid the cost of Christian discipleship. Paul therefore pleads with his readers not to be misled by such sceptics who were found in Corinth, not just in the world but, sadly, also in the church. They should remember that 'bad company corrupts good character' (15:33) and so distance themselves from false teachers in the church. In this way they would return to their senses and stop the slide into sin which those who denied the resurrection had caused (15:34).

We have surely read enough to know that the doctrine of the resurrection is not just of interest for the future, but has a huge impact on our lives in the present. If there is no future resurrection to look forward to, then we have no motivation to live any differently from those around us; but if we know that one day we will be raised with Christ, we will be spurred on to live sacrificially for him in this present world, whatever the cost. A rejection of Christian hope will lead to self-indulgence, but those who hold to the gospel will have the motivation they need to live with self-control and 'stop sinning' (15:34).

The resurrection body

Paul is aware that some sceptics will still not be convinced by his argument so far, and he imagines one asking, 'How are the dead raised? With what kind of body will they come?' (15:35). Many Christians have asked similar questions: 'What kind of body will we have in the new creation?' 'Will we be recognizable?' 'Will I be in my forty-five-year-old prime?' Those are perfectly reasonable questions for a believer to ask, but it is clear from the opening of Paul's response in verse 36 that he imagines the question of the previous verse on the lips of a hardened cynic, not a confused Christian. Here is someone who finds Paul's teaching laughable: 'Come off it Paul,' he says, 'You don't really expect us to believe in the idea of a resurrection body, do you? It's ridiculous! A corpse soon rots away or is burnt to ashes, how can it possibly receive a body again?' Paul responds vigorously: 'How foolish!' (15:36). It is the cynic, not the apostle, who is not thinking straight, as he is ignoring the ample evidence that supports Paul's assertion that there is such a thing as a resurrection body.

In outlining this evidence, Paul begins by pointing to nature. The natural world provides examples of life from death for, as Paul points out, 'What you sow does not come to life unless it dies' (15:36). We do not put a whole plant in the ground, but rather a seed. It looks so lifeless, even dead, but what comes out is very different. This remarkable transformation has been caused by God who gives the seed a body (15:38). It is the sceptics' ignorance of God (15:34) that causes their folly, as it is the fool who 'says in his heart, "There is no God"' (Psalm 14:1). If they would only open their eyes to see what God is already doing in nature, they would not find it difficult to believe what he will do at the end of time, when he gives departed Christians new resurrection bodies.

Nature not only provides examples of life from death, but also of different kinds of body. As Paul points out, 'All flesh is not the same: Men have one kind of flesh, animals have another, birds another and fish another' (15:39). The same variety is found in the heavenly bodies (15:41). If we can recognize that God has already created many varieties of body, both on earth and in the heavens, we should not find it hard to accept that he can create two different kinds of human body: the earthly body we have now and the resurrection body we will receive in the future.

Our present bodies are perishable, dishonourable and weak (15:42–43). Perhaps you are especially conscious of that as you see your hair turning grey or falling out, and find your limbs do not move quite so nimbly as they used to. The world is horrified by such bodily decay and spends large sums of money trying to delay or disguise it, but Christians have a hope that will enable them to cope with the frustrations and indignities of ageing. We know that one day we will receive

202 | TRUE SPIRITUALITY

a new body that is imperishable, glorious and powerful (15:42–43).

I vividly remember an older saint hobbling slowly into church one Sunday. With a smile she said, 'You don't know where I can find some new legs, do you?' I replied, 'Yes I do, but you may have to wait a while. You'll get them when Jesus comes again.' Immediately she exclaimed, 'That's worth waiting for!'

A spiritual body

Having mentioned evidence from the natural world to support such faith, Paul now points to the risen body of Jesus himself as evidence that there is a 'spiritual' as well as a 'natural' body (15:44b). Any suggestion that a body could be spiritual would have been shocking to some in Corinth who believed that matter belonged to this world and would have no part in God's final salvation. However, Paul wants them to understand that Christians will have a 'spiritual body', by which he means a supernatural rather than an immaterial one, in the new creation. To make his point, he speaks again of Adam and Christ. Just as we all bear the likeness of our first ancestor, Adam, and have an earthly natural body like his, so one day those who belong to Christ will bear his likeness and receive a heavenly spiritual body (15:45–49). We are not told precisely what form it will take, although we can assume that, just as the disciples recognized the risen Christ, so our new bodies will be in recognizable continuity with our earthly ones and yet be transformed. They will certainly be physical. The new creation will not be the bland immaterial existence of disembodied souls floating in nothingness that some imagine it to be. It will rather be a physical place, populated by people with material bodies in the awesome presence of God.

I was having my hair cut one day when my barber, who enjoys philosophical discussions, raised the question of life after death. After a brief conversation he said, 'The trouble is, nobody has ever come back from the dead to tell us what it's like.' Even a nervous evangelist like me could not miss that opportunity! I was able to tell him about Christ who had died and rose again. His resurrection is the guarantee that there is hope beyond the grave. If we trust in him, we can always have something to look forward to, even if we lose family, friends and physical capacity in this world. One mark of godly Christians as they get older is that they do not just live in the past, like so many elderly people, but are looking forward to the future. The Christian can always say, 'The best is still to come.'

A defeated enemy

Paul now brings us right to the end of this present age and to the fulfilment of God's saving purposes. Our earthly 'perishable' bodies can have no place in God's 'imperishable' kingdom in the new creation (15:50), so God must replace them. Paul describes what will happen, in words that anyone familiar with Handel's *Messiah* will want to sing; Christians, whether living or dead, 'will all be changed – in a flash, in the twinkling of an eye, at the last trumpet' (15:51–52). Then, at last, the prophecy will be fulfilled: 'Death has been swallowed up in victory' (15:54).

Death is a terrible enemy and at the moment it looks as if he is winning. As every day passes, taking us closer to the grave, it is as if we can hear him whispering in our ear, 'I'll get you in the end.' He taunts us in the appearance of every grey hair or wrinkle, and no amount of Grecian 2000 or Botox can silence him. As the years go by, he seems to say to us, 'It won't be long, you'll be mine any day now' and, as we see the coffin of our loved one lowered into the earth or heading for an incinerator, his grip on us can appear both firm and final. But the Christian need not cower as we listen to death's attempts to intimidate us. We can answer back and taunt him, 'Where, O death, is your victory? Where, O death is your sting?' (15:55).

The late David Watson, an evangelist, sometimes illustrated what happened when Jesus died by telling of a day when he was summoned to the garden by the terrified cries of his daughter, who was being pursued by a bee. He wrapped his arms round her and, moments later, she felt his body tense. He then let her go, saying, 'You needn't worry now, darling, the bee has stung me and bees don't sting twice.'

That story helps us understand the assurance we can have now that Christ has died. We deserve to face the sting of God's condemnation because of our sin, but it was as if the Lord Jesus wrapped himself around us as he died on the cross and faced the penalty in our place, so we need not face it. We may still die, but what Paul calls 'the sting of death' (15:56) has been drawn. Death is nothing to fear because Christ has defeated him. 'Thanks be to God! He gives us the victory through our Lord Jesus Christ' (15:57).

Stand firm!

Paul concludes this magnificent chapter with a final appeal. He pleads with the Corinthians, 'Stand firm. Let nothing move you.' That was a plea to them not to be shaken by those who denied the resurrection of the dead. We too must be on our guard against any dilution of Christianity from a gospel of salvation from sin into the offer of an experience focused entirely in the present as a form of spiritual lifestyle accessory.

We must never accept a corruption of the gospel, but stick firmly to the authentic faith that was prophesied in the Old Testament Scriptures and entrusted to the apostles, 'that Christ died for our sins according to the Scriptures, that he was buried, that he was raised on the third day according to the Scriptures' (15:3–4).

Paul says, 'Always give yourselves fully to the work of the Lord, because you know that your labour in the Lord is not in vain' (15:58). If the first half of the verse is chiefly an appeal to the Corinthians to hold firmly to the hope of future resurrection, the second half calls on them to walk the way of the cross. By claiming to enjoy the full experience of risen life now, some in Corinth had sought to bypass that road. They were not interested in battling against sin or putting themselves out for others, but were focused only on maximizing their spiritual experience. They scorned Paul as weak and could not understand why he lived such an impoverished life in the service of the gospel. His labours seemed such a waste of effort when he could have been enjoying spiritual ecstasy with them, but Paul knew that his hard work was not futile. He understood that true spirituality meant walking now in Christ's footsteps on the way of the cross, with the certain hope of one day being raised with him in glory.

Many will think us foolish if we devote ourselves wholeheartedly to following Christ. At times we ourselves may even wonder if they are right, when the cost is great and we face real hardship because of our faithfulness to our Lord. At such times we should remember his own example of loving sacrifice on the cross and his resurrection from the dead. The battles and hardships of this present world will not last for ever. One day the trumpets will sound, marking the end of this present age and the beginning of the perfect eternal age to come. Then, at last, we will enjoy all the fruits of the victory Christ won on the cross. Armed with the assurance of this great hope, we can resolve to obey Paul's final appeal: 'Always give yourselves fully to the work of the Lord, because you know that your labour in the Lord is not in vain' (15:58).

Bible study (1 Corinthians 15)

15:1–11

1. What was the gospel Paul had preached to the Corinthians?

15:12–19

2. What are the implications if Christ was not raised?

15:20–34

3. What are the consequences of the fact that he has been raised (verses 20–28)?
4. How should that affect how you live now (verses 29–34)?

15:35–49

5. What will the resurrection body be like?

15:50–58

6. What can you look forward to in the future?
7. Why is that an encouragement to 'give [ourselves] fully to the work of the Lord' (verse 58)?
8. What will that look like in practice?

Finally . . .

9. What have you learnt about true spirituality?
10. What alternative thinking does this challenge?

Epilogue

Hearing the challenge

There is a danger, given our debates about the ministry of the Spirit, that we read a book called *True Spirituality* simply to see what line it takes on the more contentious issues. We then consign both it and the author to one of the boxes we have in our minds: Pentecostal, Charismatic, extreme Charismatic, conservative, mega-conservative or balanced (often a category in which we place only ourselves). We will then, depending on which box we have chosen, either dismiss the book or enjoy its confirmation of our prejudices and think to ourselves, 'That's just what that other lot need to hear.' That would not only be a descent into the very factionalism which Paul is so critical of in Corinth, but also a failure to hear the challenge of God's word ourselves.

The Christian is called not to 'grieve the Holy Spirit' (Ephesians 4:30), but to 'keep in step with the Spirit' (Galatians 5:25). Paul's teaching in 1 Corinthians helps us understand what that will look like in practice. The apostle challenges our limited focus on just a few aspects of the Spirit's ministry and shows his concern to lead us into godliness in all of life.

Ask yourself the following questions:

1. In what ways have you, like the Corinthians, drifted from the paths of true spirituality?
2. Have you begun to lose your focus on 'Christ and him crucified' (2:2) and to look instead to human wisdom and human leaders?
3. Do you need to repent of a permissive approach to morality which is careless about sin?
4. Have you become so obsessed with yourself, your rights and your gifts, that you have little concern for the impact of your behaviour on others?
5. Are you so focused on living for the present that you hardly think about the glorious future you have to look forward to, and are therefore not prepared to make sacrifices now in the light of it?

Does the Holy Spirit have me?

My study of the New Testament at the time of my spiritual crisis as a young man assured me that, along with all who had trusted in Christ, the Holy Spirit was living in my life. That is a wonderful truth, but it is certainly not an excuse for complacency. I may have the Holy Spirit, but does the Holy Spirit have me?

Notes

Acknowledgments

1 Francis Schaeffer, *True Spirituality* (Wheaton, Illinois: Tyndale House Publishers, 2001).

Introduction

1 David Jackman, *Let's Study 1 Corinthians* (Edinburgh: Banner of Truth, 2004), pp. xi–xii.

2 David Jackman, *Let's Study 1 Corinthians* (Edinburgh: Banner of Truth, 2004).

3 David E. Garland, *1 Corinthians* (Grand Rapids, Michigan: Baker Academic, 2008).

Chapter 1

1 John Stott, *The Cross of Christ: 20th Anniversary Edition* (Nottingham: Inter-Varsity Press, 2006), p. 32.

2 Richard Dawkins, *The God Delusion* (London: Bantam Press, 2006), p. 253.

Chapter 2

1 Joseph Hart, 1759.

2 This illustration comes from John Stott's excellent exposition of the opening chapters of 1 Corinthians. John Stott, *Calling Christian Leaders* (Leicester: Inter-Varsity Press, 2002), p. 41.

3 R. Kent Hughes and Barbara Hughes, *Liberating Ministry from the Success Syndrome* (Wheaton, Illinois: Crossway, 2008), p. 43.

4 R. Kent Hughes and Barbara Hughes, *Liberating Ministry from the Success Syndrome* (Wheaton, Illinois: Crossway, 2008), p. 35.

Chapter 3

1 *Sunday Times*, 2 September 2007.

2 John Blanchard, *Does God Believe in Atheists?* (Darlington: Evangelical Press, 2000), p. 201.

3 You might find the chapter on homosexuality helpful in my book, *Battles Christians Face*: Vaughan Roberts, *Battles Christians Face* (Milton Keynes: Authentic Lifestyle, 2007).

4 Quoted in the Evangelical Alliance Symposium, 'The 18–30 Mission', 16 September 2009.

5 See, for example, www.covenanteyes.com

Chapter 4

1 Genesis 1:27–28; Genesis 2:20–25; Ephesians 5:22–33. For more detail see: Christopher Ash, *Married for God* (Nottingham: Inter-Varsity Press, 2007).

Chapter 5

1 Haddon Robinson, *Decision-Making by the Book* (Wheaton, Illinois: Scripture Press, 1992), p. 151.

2 This diagram is based on a similar one in *Decision Making and the Will of God* by Garry Friesen (Portland, Oregon: Multnomah Books, 1980), p. 179.

3 J. I. Packer, *Laid-back Religion?* (Nottingham: Inter-Varsity Press, 1987), p. 80.

4 See 1 Corinthians 4:6, 18, 19; 5:2; 8:1; 13:4 and Colossians 2:18.

5 Quoted in E. Kevan, *The Lord's Supper* (Darlington: Evangelical Press, 1966), p. 22.

6 J. Hardyman, *Idols: God's Battle for our Hearts* (Nottingham: Inter-Varsity Press, 2010), p. 21.

Chapter 6

1 John Gray, *Men Are from Mars, Women Are from Venus: A Practical Guide for Improving Communication and Getting What You Want in Your Relationships* (New York: HarperCollins, 1993).

2 Simone de Beauvoir, *The Second Sex* (London: Vintage, 1997), p. 295.

3 Shirley Conran, *Superwoman* (London: Penguin, 1975).

4 David Jackman, *Let's Study 1 Corinthians* (Edinburgh: Banner of Truth, 2004), pp. 182–183.

5 Karl Marx and Friedrich Engels, *The Communist Manifesto* (London: Penguin, 2002).

6 George Orwell, *Animal Farm* (London: Penguin, 1996), p. 133.

7 Words taken from the 'Prayer of Humble Access' in the Anglican Book of Common Prayer.

8 Lindsay Brown, *Shining Like Stars: The Power of the Gospel in the World's Universities* (Nottingham: Inter-Varsity Press, 2007), p. 133–134.

9 Francis Schaeffer, *The Mark of the Christian* (London: Inter-Varsity Press, 1971), p. 13.

Chapter 7

1 For example, in verse 4 and elsewhere he uses the word *charisma*, from which we get the word 'Charismatic'.

2 Romans 12:4–8; Ephesians 4:11; and 1 Peter 4:10–11.

3 Anthony C. Thiselton, *The First Epistle to the Corinthians* (Grand Rapids: Eerdmans, 2000), pp. 936–989.

4 Vaughan Roberts, *True Worship* (Carlisle, Cumbria: Authentic Lifestyle, 2002), pp. 75–76.

5 John Stott, *Baptism and Fullness* (Leicester: IVP, 1975), p. 36.

Chapter 8

1 C. S. Lewis, *Miracles* (London & Glasgow: Collins/Fontana, 1947, Revised 1960), p. 153.